DANCE
CHILDREN
DANCE

Dance, Children, Dance

JIM RAYBURN III

Tyndale House Publishers, Inc.
WHEATON, ILLINOIS

ACKNOWLEDGMENTS

My special thanks to Lucia, Shannon, and
Michelle, who gave so much and asked for so lit-
tle, and without whose love, faith, and support
this project would not have been possible.
   To Wally and Judy Urban, Dick Halverson, Bill
and Bea Mitchell, William and Marge Andrews,
Donna Johnson, Elsie Lane, Bill Taylor, Wendell
Hawley, Ken Petersen, Tim Botts, and Tyndale
House Publishers—a most heartfelt thank-you.
Your various contributions to this very personal
goal will not be forgotten.

Material taken from *He That Is Spiritual,* copyright 1918 by Lewis Sperry Chafer, copyright
1967 by Zondervan Publishing House, is used
by permission.

Quotations taken from *He That Is Spiritual* by
Lewis Sperry Chafer, copyright 1918 by Lewis
Sperry Chafer, copyright 1967 by Zondervan Pub-
lishing House, are used by permission.

First printing, October 1984

TO **JIM,**
WHOSE COMPASSION,
WARMTH, HUMOR, WIT,
RUGGED INDIVIDUALISM,
AND RAGING LOVE AFFAIR
WITH DEITY
ARE ALL TOO SELDOM
SEEN.

ALSO TO **MAXINE,**
FOR HER HONESTY,
SENSITIVITY,
AND WILLINGNESS
TO EXPOSE THE DEPTH
OF HER OWN STRUGGLES
THAT THE TRUTH
MAY BE TOLD.
KEEP DANCING, KID.

CONTENTS

FOREWORD

JIM RAYBURN was one of the few authentic heroes in my life. From our first meeting to the last, he was for me the prototype of what a servant of Christ should be. He relished life. His gutsy courage was legendary. His ability to communicate the love of God in Christ was simply incomparable. His spontaneous humor, which seemed always to lie very near the surface, was never irrelevant or out of place. Its sheer naturalness was always integral to his speech, the antithesis of the sort of artificial humor that is dragged in to get a laugh or is used for the sake of comedy relief.

More often than not, Jim made his point in ways that evoked sheer delight and profound insight simultaneously. He was the master iconoclast who was totally unimpressed with pretension and pomposity. He was the incarnation of God's love in Christ, and he communicated that love in attitude and action as well as in word. His devotion to Christ was contagious.

Biographers sometimes go to one extreme or the other especially when the subject is a next of kin. The subject is portrayed as a saint, whose life was above criticism, virtually infallible, one with whom the reader is unable to identify. Or the subject is portrayed as a character without virtue, one in whom the reader would find little, if anything, to emulate.

Jim Rayburn III has avoided both extremes. He simply records facts about a father and mother who struggled, often with questionable success, to nurture their marriage and family. It is the story of a devoted couple who suffered almost beyond belief and human endurance. Despite this, they remained true to Christ and to one another.

Here is the record of a pilgrimage with Christ which will inspire, instruct, awe, amaze, and motivate its readers. Congratulations as you embark on this unforgettable adventure.

Richard C. Halverson
Chaplain, United States Senate
July 18, 1984

ONE
Roots

IMITATING his traveling evangelist father, young Jim, age two and a half, looked down from the tabletop on which he was standing, shook his finger in the air, and struggled for the words, "All be good. All be good!" The guests who had gathered for this performance laughed and nodded their approval. Young "Jamie" seemed destined to make a fine preacher-man, his parent's choice of all possible professions.

Outside of school, Jim's early life was centered around the First Presbyterian Church in Newton, Kansas. Life was an endless routine of Sunday school meetings, church camps, youth group gatherings, Bible studies, choir practices, and prayer meetings. For a live wire like Jim, it must have been a little dull.

Sunday was a holy day in Jim's household; one was not permitted to read, work, or play until Monday arrived. The only book one could read on Sunday was the Bible. Since work was not allowed, meals for the holy day were prepared on Saturday. Playing any kind of game, and there were very few that weren't considered sinful, was strictly forbidden. Jim was finally allowed to play catch with a baseball (after much family discussion), but there was to be no hitting, no running, and no shouting. Using the bat to hit the ball was absolutely forbidden, a breach of God's ways. Having fun on holy day required punishment, which served to appease an angry God. Come Monday, however, God himself became a baseball fan. One could play all the baseball he had time for, and with God's blessing to boot.

To Jim the whole concept of divine goodness was lost in the drudgery of religion. God seemed to be a narrow-minded antagonist, rather than a spiritual being whose very essence is love. Nevertheless, it was called the "Christian life," and Jim was expected to follow it.

Jim's mother could have doubled for Carrie Nation (one of her heroines) or perhaps a United States Marine Corps recruiter. What she lacked in physical stature was made up for in rigid personality. Not known for possessing tolerance or patience, she viewed any kind of weakness as sin.

Mother Rayburn was very competitive, and taught her children to be competitive too. She rose extra early on Tuesday mornings to be the first woman on the block to have her laundry hanging on the clothesline. It seemed important to her that the other housewives made note of her victory. She taught them the

"Christian" way on laundry day. It was based on the belief that God loves a hard worker far more than one who sleeps an extra hour.

Jim's parents had themselves been products of very strict, religious upbringings. His mother had come from a home where those who knocked on the door were greeted with a verse of Scripture. For her, childhood had contained little love, and absolutely no freedom. Words of love were simply mixed with dutiful obligations, and then presented to the children under the label of Christianity. Although a pretty package to the senses, the candy inside was poison.

By constitution and conviction, Jim was unable to reproduce the kind of joyless Christianity his parents favored. But like many other children so instructed, Jim grew up with a ton of guilt in his backpack. It was a heavy load to carry, and for most of his life he struggled with the weight of it, for it's difficult to dance with too much weight in one's pack.

Young Jim was not to be known as a preacher-man; in both his appearance and his approach to discipleship he had no regard for the traditional role. Nor did he arrive at "being good," at least not in the external sense of his parents' understanding. But his was a life that influenced thousands, and deeply affected my own. There are those who feel Jim was a prophet, and others say a saint. Some have called him a sinner, a dreamer, and a revolutionary. I called him Dad.

13

A quest for high adventure followed Jim throughout his life, and seasoned every aspect of it. It seems he split, cracked, or shattered every other bone in his body in pursuit of excitement, be it challenging the white water rapids, exploring an abandoned mine, hanging by rope to the side of a cliff, ditching a policeman in a highway chase, or jumping off a windswept cornice to a vertical snowfield far below. When asked if he had any regard for his safety, Jim always replied, "My activities are just as safe as sitting in church—probably safer."

That such a man would make his mark upon the world with a spiritual legacy seems too good to be true, for he resembled a man of the cloth about as much as Marilyn Monroe resembled the Islam concept of "woman of the year." But to those who couldn't relate to religion, or religionists, Jim was a dashing individual—the "James Bond" of ministers.

Much of Jim's adult life was to be lived in conflict, however. The battle to separate the insights in his heart from the ways of his folks would be a long and difficult ordeal. To follow his heart and ignore the rules was to jeopardize his standing with God. To accept the ways of his parents, however, was to make a mockery of God within his own heart. "The problem with me," Jim would later express, "is that I got starched and ironed before I got washed."

It is said that truth is stranger than fiction. The story of Jim's life will support that. He was a man who had a love affair with Jesus Christ, a man who pioneered a revolutionary movement within an often stagnant religious system, and a man whose warmth and love inspired thousands. Yet, he would die in dehumanizing pain, rejected by many of the people he loved most.

14 His story begins with Helen Maxine Stanley, a pretty woman with a soft heart and a free spirit.

T W O Romance

UNLIKE Jim's family, whose entire life was a progression of evangelistic meetings, Maxine's folks had been merry Irish rebels from the Catholic church who turned every meeting into a frolic. Max grew up with unlimited freedom to do as she pleased. Even as a young child, she was allowed to leave the house and spend the day alone in the streets of Kansas City. Her parents struggled with a dying marriage, and she was largely ignored.

When Max was fourteen, her life was dramatically altered. Returning from school, she found a note from her mother on the piano bench:

> *Dear Max,*
> *I've gone away. Don't try to find me.*
>
> *Mom*

How is a child to understand such a note? Perceiving herself to be unwanted and unloved, Max never again felt secure, safe, and appreciated. Her self-image was shattered; life was now a matter of survival.

Max was first sent to the home of her mother's sister. While lying in bed at night, she could overhear the conversations in the living room. Much of what she heard was painful—"What shall we do with Maxine? We can't shoot her."

Shuffled from home to home, Max was not to find acceptance. Abandoned by her mother, unwanted by others, she felt the deep, searing pain of a broken heart. To escape her pain, Max made up fantasies in which she was wanted and appreciated. No fantasy was sweeter than that of meeting the prince who would take her away from her miserable existence, away to his castle where he would love and cherish her forever.

It was a strange twist of destiny that led Jim's path across Maxine's. She was a street urchin from the city; he was a small-town church-boy. His family was stable but restrictive; hers, though once fun loving, was now broken and dispersed. Jim was happy, positive, and assertive; Max was unhappy, skeptical, and timid. In almost every way they were opposites.

Maxine met Jim at a concert. She rarely went to church, but that night she had gone to the First Presbyterian Church in Concordia, Kansas, at the request of a friend. The College of Emporia Glee Club was performing, and many of its members—Jim included—were seeking dates.

Jim saw Max in the audience and fell for her immediately. During the performance he pointed her out to a friend and insisted that this was the girl he would marry. Max recalls: "As soon as the service was over I went to the foyer to await the arrival of the glee club. Soon, this very handsome young man came running up to me, offered his hand and said, 'Hi, my name is Jim Rayburn, what's yours?' There was something in his style that swept me off my feet. He was warm, friendly, and confident.

"We spent the rest of the evening in a little cafe, eating peanuts, drinking Coke, and talking. The next morning Jim picked me up in a taxi and took me to school. You can't imagine the reaction of my classmates when I showed up in a taxi cab." On this cold, seemingly uneventful night in Concordia, Kansas, Maxine found her prince. She was a senior in high school, Jim a sophomore at the College of Emporia. The date was January 13, 1929.

The young couple wasted no time arranging to study together that Fall at Kansas State University. Maxine, a talented artist, had hoped to pursue an art career. To pacify her father, however, who thought all artists were bums, she selected home economics as a major.

University life was good for both. Max was a member of the Tri Delta sorority, Jim the Pi Kappa Alpha fraternity. They had each other, they were busy, and life was good. Max was elected the campus beauty queen her freshman year, a tremendous affirmation for a girl who had been unwanted and ignored. This year at K.S.U. was an emotional banquet for a very lonely girl.

Jim was dating the prettiest girl on campus and was proud as a peacock. That same year he was elected president of his fraternity. His parents, who thought that fraternities were educational organizations, were proud that their son had received such an honor. Little did they know what another world he had entered.

17

Jim was a born leader as well as a born ham, a cross between General Patton and Will Rogers. He was always at the head of the parade. Sometimes he was really leading, other times just showing off, but he was always in the spotlight.

At the College of Emporia, Jim had decided to play football. It didn't go so well. He was rugged and could hold his own on a mountain trail with a goat, but contact sports were not his forte. As he later summed up his football career: "I was fed to the varsity four times a week; they just made hamburger out of me. Many are the times I awoke in the shower."

Not one to be dismayed, Jim always found another way to go if his original plans faltered. Since his football career wasn't going anywhere, he decided to try cheerleading at Kansas State. He made it, too. So at every sporting event that came along, Jim led the troops and directed the band.

These were the Depression years, and times were hard. Because of financial shortages, Max was unable to return for her sophomore year. She went back to her stepmother's house in Concordia, and Jim returned to the university to complete his studies. They were together whenever possible.

Upon graduation, Jim headed for a summer of study at the University of Colorado in Boulder. While he was there, a fraternity brother phoned to inform him that Max had been seen with another man. Jim had a mortal fear of losing her, and this was no small threat. As soon as school was out, he headed home and went straight to see her. On September 11, 1932, before a justice of the peace in Harrisonville, Missouri, they married.

In Jim's mind, eloping would hold Maxine while he figured out how to manage his parents. He had several problems with which to contend. In the first place, he was scared to death of his folks. Second, by eloping he had smeared the family name and insulted God Almighty, as they were later to inform him. Further, Max was not the kind of girl the Rayburn family held in the highest regard. The four Rayburn boys were expected to choose their wives from the nearest chapter of the Women's Christian Temperance Union, or something similar. Max hardly fit the mold. In the Rayburns' eyes, she may as well have been raised by wolves.

There was another problem, a different kind of problem that no one could see. A few days before marrying Maxine, Jim had offered his life to God. Jim had no idea what this might mean, and Max didn't grasp it either when he told her, sometime after the wedding ceremony in Harrisonville. Jim remembered his commitment like this:

Out of engineering school, I went to graduate school at Colorado University to specialize in mineralogy. While I was up there I got miserable, like lots of Christians who've been out of touch with the Lord do. One of the things the Lord used to bring me back to myself was a sense of futility and misery. Often I was spending as high as eighteen hours a day in the mineralogy lab, just because I loved to monkey around with rocks. Yet I was unhappy way down deep. Well, I went up on a mountain one night and told the Lord I was sick and tired of the mess I'd made of my life. If he wanted to take over, he could do so. I did the best I knew, in my stumbling way, to take hands off. Believe me, when anybody does that, I don't care how stumbling and blundering they are, the Lord will take them up on it!

All alone on a mountainside in Boulder, Colorado, a young man cried out to his heavenly Father, made an offering of his life, and unknowingly set in motion a revolution in the course of twentieth-century Christianity. But in 1932, neither Jim nor Maxine realized what had taken place.

19

Standing before the justice of the peace, Max had
no idea that Jim would take her back to Concordia.
She had finally married her prince, only to find he
wasn't taking her away. Greatly depressed by this turn
of events, she returned to her job and waited for Jim
to inform his folks. She was doubtful that he would.
Ever since her mother left her, Max had struggled
with a pessimistic outlook. It was hard for her to believe that anyone would love her permanently. But
Jim was always positive and upbeat. Two months after
their secret wedding, he wrote:

Maxie, my darling,
I've tried so often to encourage you, both by letter
and in person. On almost every occasion I've met with
such failure that I hesitate to make the attempt again.
But I shall make one more attempt at showing you the
bright side of this gloomy situation, despite past fail-
ures, and I shall make every promise that is humanly
possible regarding our future.
Oh, Maxie, my precious little wife, how my heart has
gone out for you since your last two letters arrived. I'd
have given a million dollars to have been there when
your folks were indulging in all the criticism and
thoughtless, inexcusable kidding. Oh, honey, I know it
was hard for you. I long to be near you Maxie, and
fight your battles for you, and let your heartaches be
my heartaches too, as they always are.
Today your letter is full of the blues, worrying about
having your job after Christmas. Honey, you won't
need your job after Christmas. You don't have to worry
about getting fired; you're going to quit. Darling,
you're going to be with me! Now, my precious, does the
job amount to anything?
I have decided to wait until this series of meetings is
over to tell Dad. He needs me badly here and might
consider it a most inopportune time to announce a se-

20

*cret marriage. You see, I don't know his viewpoint, and
I can't discern it, so this is my only course to safeguard
his work and insure my present usefulness to him. So,
dear kid, these meetings will close two weeks from next
Monday. Immediately thereafter I shall "blow the
works" to fond parents. You better have your ear close
to the phone to get the outcome right from "ringside." It
is going to be the hardest job of my life. I don't know
how I'll do it, but I will, don't ever doubt that. I've got
to utterly destroy the folks' confidence in me and build
it back again, all in the same session.*

*Now, honey-mine, just think, very soon I'll have you
and you'll have me. Honestly darling, no sacrifice
would seem great, or nothing hard to give up, if I can
have you near me and make you happy. It may be
hard, dear, it may be a fight to exist for a while, but
we'll have each other and we'll be fighting side by side.
Come what may, we'll have our love and we'll have
God ever near us. Honey, isn't that enough to make
you glad you're alive, anxious to live, and happy, in
spite of any trials you are put to?*

*Now, sweet kid, I want you to be happy. We belong
to each other, and the rest of the world can go hang to
a sour apple tree. I love you, Maxie. Nothing else matters. So, my sweet baby, just consider yourself forever
loved, and stop worrying.*

21

*Your own,
"Jimmie," forever*

Two weeks later Jim broke the news to his folks. It
was not well received. They somehow believed that
Max and Jim were "living in sin." Arrangements were
hastily made for another wedding ceremony, to be
held in the Rayburn home. The day after Christmas,
1932, the young lovers were married for the second
time. Max thought the whole thing truly ridiculous,
but Jim was still very much under his parents' author-

ity, and their word was usually final.

Right after Christmas, Jim's father held a series of evangelistic meetings in Seminole, Oklahoma. Jim had planned to take Maxine along on the six-week trip as sort of a belated honeymoon. He had told her his plans, and she was looking forward to the time with her new husband. But unfortunately for Jim and Max, his folks decided Max should stay behind and run the household. This would allow mother Rayburn to take the trip. Maxine spent only four days and nights with her prince before he hit the road.

For the next fourteen months the newlyweds stayed at the Rayburn home in Newton, Kansas. Jim was usually on the road assisting his father; Max stayed behind to help her mother-in-law.

Maxine had had no church training to speak of in her formative years, and she was somewhat self-conscious about it. She looked upon Jim's folks as the "gurus" of all matters spiritual. Naturally, she wanted to learn what she could from them. Almost overnight she found herself in every church service, Women's Christian Temperance Union meeting, Bible study, prayer meeting, and Sunday school class that was scheduled.

22

In spite of her lack of formal Christian training, Maxine was a sensitive and loving type who would freely spend her last nickel to feed a hungry cat. Full of generosity and helpfulness toward anyone who was in trouble or had a need, this young woman was refreshingly simple and real. She wore no masks, and she accepted all people. Now she found herself in a situation where love was often discussed, but infrequently shown. This was the "Christian life," she was told.

In those tough Depression years many were suffering. One day a hobo called at the Rayburn home. Maxine ran to the door, opened it wide, and was momentarily stunned; in front of her was a cold, thin man with unshaven face, feet wrapped with burlap bags, his deep sunken eyes staring into hers. He hadn't eaten in days, was desperately hungry, and was looking for work. Inviting the man to sit down and wait, Max ran to the bedroom and found a pair of Jim's shoes, tucked them under her arm and headed for the kitchen. She hastily prepared sandwiches, grabbed an apple, and returned to the living room.

As the old man departed and Maxine closed the door behind him, Mother Rayburn made her entrance, exclaiming, "Oh, Maxine, he didn't deserve a thing from us! Didn't you see he was sucking on a ciga- rette?"

Maxine would struggle for years to understand such incidents. "If a person has love in his heart," she reasoned, "how can he possibly turn a deaf ear to the suffering of any living creature? How can it possibly be wrong to help somebody? Why do I have to go to boring meetings and sit around with stone-faced people? Is this what God is like? Am I really supposed to give a hoot whether or not someone smokes, drinks, or dances? What if I don't care—does that make me evil?" Countless questions flooded her mind. It wasn't easy to find answers, because she looked upon Jim's people as model Christians. Theirs was the way that led to Christ and salvation, she was told.

Tragically, Jim was unaware of the conflict brewing within his young wife. Although he feared his parents, he didn't take their narrow ways as seriously as she did. He and his brother Paul, for example, were excellent card players, and both were known to pick up spare change utilizing card skills. Card playing was on the top ten sins list in the Rayburn home. There was one exception, however, a game called Rook. The two brothers developed a way to play bridge with Rook cards. Telling their mother they had invented a new,

23

more exciting version of Rook, they taught her to play bridge. She loved the game so much she told people all over town about it—she even gave a few lessons of her own.

Unfortunately, Max didn't have the ability to make a game of all the legalism; it really confused her. At the point in her life when she was eager to know the great mysteries of Christ, she was handed a set of rules and regulations. No emphasis was put on inward growth; only external behavior seemed to matter.

Max was not told that Christ never turned his back on someone because he or she smoked, drank, wore make-up, had a short hemline, rode fast camels, played cards or read *Cosmopolitan* magazine (the Jerusalem version). She was never told that only selfishness, self-righteousness, and pride can separate us from the Father.

Maxine was not by nature a legalistic person, but she lacked the strength to follow her own intuitions. Faced with this new, religious way of approaching life, she was unable to argue against it, as she knew very little about the Bible, church people, or Christ himself.

Although Jim was unaware of Max's deep inner conflict, he could see she wasn't very happy. In February of 1934, he was offered a job with the Presbyterian Board of National Missions in New Mexico. The young couple saw this as an opportunity to start their life anew, away from parents and in-laws. They enthusiastically accepted the job and, in March, headed for the great Southwest.

THREE
Country Pastor

CHAMA, New Mexico, was Jim's kind of place, but to Maxine it felt like the outer limit of civilization. Max had never been a robust, outdoor type of person. She wasn't one to pioneer new territory or blaze a new trail. Jim, on the other hand, was constantly on the lookout for a new adventure. A wild and remote place like Chama was just his type of playground.

There was one Protestant church in Rio Arriba County; Jim was the pastor. Behind the church was the manse, a dilapidated wooden structure which served as home for the young couple. It looked like something from a ghost town, and it had no water or

electricity. The "bathroom" was a fine two-seater out-
house a short walk away; it also served as the church
restroom.

The former pastor had offended a few folks and attendance was low. The solution, Jim figured, was for
him to call on everyone in the county. Life became a
daily routine of trips into remote areas of northern
New Mexico in search of any miners, ranchers, Indi-
ans, or others who might live there. Usually Max went
along. If they could drive, they did; if there were no
adequate roads, they went by foot or on horseback.
They slept in the car, on the ground, and inside rat-
infested buildings with dirt floors. Jim loved every
minute of it, but his wife found the routine shocking
and exhausting.

Max had never wanted to be a preacher's wife in
the first place; that role didn't mesh with her personality. But Jim's degree in civil engineering had not
opened any doors to employment, so he had accepted
this job as a means of leaving Kansas. The way Max
viewed it, living in New Mexico would at least provide
them with more time to be together. It didn't pan out,
however. If Max wanted to be with Jim she had to accompany him, something she had neither the physical
strength nor emotional grit to continue. She began to
spend more time at home while Jim pursued his visita-
tions, and the seeds of discontent over Jim's increasing absence began to take root in her heart. Little did
Jim realize how much Max needed him. Being one of
four sons, he had spent little time around women and
was somewhat naïve about his wife's emotional needs.
The only woman he had had real exposure to was his
mother, who gladly kept the home fires burning while
his father was away preaching. Jim was simply following in his father's footsteps, and that's precisely what
concerned Maxine.

Max and Jim would spend less than a year in

Chama. One early spring morning, Jim was returning
from another excursion. Eager to get home, he was
pushing the speedometer a bit, as was his custom. On
the roadway ahead he noticed a car stopped on the
shoulder and a group of people looking it over. Pulling to his left to allow more room for passing, Jim
slowed his car as he approached. Without warning, an
elderly man wandered from behind the stalled car directly onto the highway. There was no time to swerve.
Jim heard the sound of screeching tires interrupted by
a sickening thud. As Jim's vehicle came to a stop, he
could hear the screams of the people behind him.
Shaking, he ran to the broken, bloodied body lying by
the roadside. Jim knelt down and took the old man in
his arms. He was still alive! Blinking back tears, Jim
struggled to his feet with the injured man in his arms
and carried him to the car. From the accident scene to
the doctor's house was both the fastest and the longest drive of Jim's life. But it was all to no avail. The
old man died before they arrived.

Outside of Maxine, Jim never told anyone about the
accident. It undeniably affected his image in the area,
however. Four of the old man's relatives came to the
house a week later and threatened to even the score.
Several very tense weeks followed, and Jim's ministry
in Chama, so enthusiastically begun, never seemed to
go as smoothly after that.

Seven months later, in January of 1935, the Board of
Missions moved the young couple to Douglas, Arizona,
a small town on the Mexican border. Jim's official
duty was to pastor the local church and establish a
program for the youngsters. Concerning his Sunday
school, the first thing he attempted, Jim would later
say, "If you want anybody to show up, don't have it on
Sunday and don't call it school." At first it surprised
him that most kids wanted no part of Sunday school.
Disliking it had not been an option for Jim. The path

27

of least resistance had been to accept the many hours spent in church, and he had never realized that kids could have strong negative feelings about it. As soon as he learned this lesson, Jim shifted the emphasis of his work with kids to activities well outside his church building. In no time, he and Max were up to their eyebrows in Cub Scout meetings, Boy Scout meetings, and camping trips.

Having grown up in a stifling religious environment where most people were less than honest, Jim was immensely attracted to open-minded and sincere people. Because they usually possess these qualities, teenage people were very special to him. Further, no group of people is more enthusiastic about life and living than high-school kids. Jim was the only adult most kids knew who shared this enthusiasm. Teenagers, even if they didn't understand most adults, had little trouble understanding Jim; he was a live wire, full of youthful enthusiasm.

Jim soon found a secret to successful work with kids—simply include them in the activities he already enjoyed. For hundreds of young people in southern Arizona, that meant outdoor camping. While they were seated around an open fire, gazing into the glorious Arizona night sky, and listening to the nearby stream, Jim would talk to them of Christ. His way of speaking was wonderfully fresh and alive. The more he talked, the more they wanted to listen.

A trademark of Jim's talks was to dare his listeners to take him seriously. In a slow drawl that sounded very much like the actor Jimmy Stewart, he would say, "Now if you think you've got something more important to think about than Jesus Christ, then you just come over here and put your little nose up against mine and tell little old Jim what you think is more important." He seldom had any takers. By the time he

sent the kids off to bed down, most of them were in
pretty deep thought. It was usually the first time these
kids had ever thought about the subject, too, as most
were long-time dropouts from anything with spiritual
or religious overtones. They hadn't come into the
woods to talk about Jesus, either, but Jim didn't look,
talk, or act like a minister, and what he had to say
was interesting. He was more like a friend, a big
brother. Maxine remembers: "Jim truly enjoyed his
work with kids, but found pastoring a church was not
his 'thing.' He hated the idea of being called *Reverend*
and would not permit people to so address him. The
pastor's image in Jim's mind was of one who was
above us mortals—one who preached long, dull sermons, and prayed long, dull prayers, always in a rhe-
torical style. Jim just didn't fit the mold; his approach
was unconventional in every way.

"I remember a time when Jim overheard some negative talk (from his own church members) about the
local Douglas, Arizona, bum. Well, the first thing Jim
did was to look up that lonely old man and issue him
a warm and special invitation to our home, as well as
the church. Jim really had a heart for people like
that—people that no one cared about. That man had
been rejected for a long time, because he was an alco-
holic."

One Sunday morning, Jim was dutifully leading the
church service when his new friend, the town drunk,
stumbled in the door and slowly shuffled up the aisle
to a seat near the pulpit. A few minutes later it was
time for the offering. A large tin can that reverberated
loudly each time a coin was dropped into it served as
the offering plate. When it came to the drunk, he
reached into his pocket and took out ten silver dollars,
raised his hand high in the air, and dropped each one
individually into the can. After this lengthy ritual of

29

◆

clang-clang-clang, the old boy staggered to his feet and slowly made his way up the aisle, never to return again.

But whenever Jim needed money for his trips with the kids, that same town drunk financed his work. Whether the need was food, sleeping bags, gasoline, or tents, the local drunk provided. The "Christian" community had treated the man with either apathy or contempt for many years, but it had never treated him with love. Jim simply offered his love and friendship to a lonely old man, and God opened up a most unexpected source of financial supply. With God as his guide, Maxine as his assistant, and the town drunk providing the resources, Jim's work with kids was booming.

The last church Jim and Max would tackle was in Clifton, Arizona, a small copper mining town several hours north of Douglas. While passing through Clifton a year before their move in October of 1935, Maxine had commented that she wouldn't be caught dead there. It was not a pretty place. "In the process of scouting out the territory," Maxine says, "Jim had met some wonderful people in Clifton who begged him to move there and work with the town's young people. Further, their little mission church had been without a pastor for some time, and they wanted Jim to take it on. I went with what I'd call 'cheerful acceptance' of the situation. I wanted to be with Jim—if that meant Siberia, then I'd have gone there."

Home in Clifton was a decrepit old wooden structure with no luxuries except for a small library. One night, while Max was at the movie theater, Jim discovered an old coverless copy of a book that would change his life. Called *He That Is Spiritual*, it was by Lewis Sperry Chafer, president of a seminary in Dallas, Texas. The book was about the Holy Spirit, grace,

and salvation. Jim had never understood these subjects as Chafer presented them.

"How misleading is the theory," Chafer wrote, "that
to be spiritual one must abandon play, diversion, and
helpful amusement. Such a conception is born of a
morbid human conscience. It is foreign to the Word of
God. It is a device of Satan to make the blessings of
God seem abhorrent to people who are overflowing
with physical life and energy. There are many who in
blindness are emphasizing negatives, giving the
impression that spirituality is opposed to joy, liberty,
and naturalness of expression in thought and life in
the Spirit. True spirituality is not a pious pose. It is not
a 'Thou shall not,' it is a 'Thou shalt.' We cannot be
normal physically, mentally, or spiritually if we neg-
lect this vital factor in human life. God has provided
that our joy shall be full."

Jim had never read anything like that before. Taboos against alcohol, games, cigarettes, make-up,
movies, sex, dancing, cards, and so on, had always
seemed irrelevant to Jim, yet he had been raised on
taboos and his parents' influence had been enormous.
He was confused, to say the least. Had not the town
drunk helped him most? Which was The Way? Chafer's book intensified the struggle. What Jim was reading was speaking to his heart like a beautiful melody,
but it challenged everything he'd been taught.

31

Although Jim had resisted many of the narrow
teachings he'd received as a child, he had never been
freed from the guilt of questioning the religious status
quo. As he read Chafer he could hardly contain his
excitement. Years later he would tell about his mo-
mentous discovery of salvation by grace:

I was a gospel preacher, I led people to the Lord Je-
sus Christ, I was a member of the Board of National
Missions of the Presbyterian Church, if you please, be-

fore I ever heard of this—the absolute finality and perfection of what Jesus Christ has done about sin.

All my life I ran scared. I remember five years in engineering school and graduate school in geology, when
all I did about my Christian life was once in a while
pray, "Now I lay me down to sleep, I pray the Lord my
soul to keep." A great big, strapping boy, a college
man, praying baby prayers.

I fooled around and left out the Lord, and all that
time I was uncomfortable about sin. I never could get
into it like my friends at the fraternity house. Oh, I had
some minor pleasures here and there, but I was always
troubled about this sin business. "Sin . . . golly, I gotta
pay for these sins." Do you ever think that? Get 'way
down deep in your insides where you're alone with
yourself and God, and you know you think, "Golly, a
person as fouled up as I am is gonna have to pay."
Well, you're not! It's been paid for.

My thinking may have never changed had not, by the
divine providence of God, I come in contact with the in-
imitable Dr. Chafer, the greatest teacher that I know of
or have read of, of the doctrine of the grace of God,
who Jesus Christ is, and what Jesus Christ has done.

I don't care if you start with the New Testament, or if
you take the Apostles' Creed or the Nicene Creed or the
Thirty-nine Articles, or what you take. Every single
creed says, "Salvation is something that God did by
himself, and we can't do anything about it." It's a package that's all wrapped up and delivered! And I know
very well that most Christians don't know that, and
don't believe it if they've heard it. And you know that
sometimes you have some doubts about it yourself.
We're all natural-born legalists.

We don't believe in the Roman ideas of going up the
steps of the cathedral on our knees, or rubbing our
nose down a 300-foot aisle that's full of dust, but we do
believe that if we're really going to be saved, then we're

going to have to pull up our socks and get going, keeping a bunch of rules. And every time we do that, we get the human element into the perfection of what Jesus Christ has already done.

Dr. Chafer's book had spoken straight to Jim's heart, and he opened his heart's door to receive the risen Christ. Jim had stepped into the realm of the Spirit one dark and quiet night as he read by the light of a candle, and as the candle's light faded away in the dawn of a new day, Jim knew the great Seeker had found him.

33

FOUR
Seminary

THERE was a new fire in Jim's spirit, a new
soaring in his soul, a freedom he had never known
before. The Creator had touched him at the point of
his own inadequacies and had not punished him. This
was called *grace,* and for Jim it was a whole new
realm of understanding.

Aware that he was uneducated in spiritual matters,
Jim sensed a deep need for further theological studies. He had not yet learned that the Holy Spirit would
be his teacher. Jim decided to pursue a seminary education. Having come from a line of Calvinists, Jim was
excited as he dropped his application to Princeton

Seminary in the Clifton, Arizona, mailbox. He and Max proceeded with plans for their move to New Jersey. They weren't concerned about his being accepted, as he had a distinguished academic record in both high school and college, as well as a long list of extracurricular activities on his records.

Finally the long-awaited letter from Princeton arrived. Jim was shocked to read, "Application Rejected." The letter explained that Jim wasn't viewed as the proper material to be a Presbyterian minister. The problem, as they saw it at Princeton, was his heavy interest in the sciences. Years later, this became an embarrassment to the folks at Princeton; one of the school's respected presidents, John A. McKay, would later refer to Jim as one of the great saints of this century.

Having been turned down by Princeton, Jim and Max were in a quandary. Summer was almost over and classes were starting soon, regardless of which school they chose. Two options were left: a small Presbyterian school in California and Dallas Seminary in Texas. Some financial aid was available if they went to California; not a dime if they chose Texas. But when the debating was over, the decision was for Dallas and L. S. Chafer, author of the book that had opened Jim's eyes.

The years in the Southwest had been good, although they were not without struggles and heartache. Jim and Max had lost two children through miscarriage, feared for their lives in Chama, and struggled with the poverty of Depression days. But these years had given them an opportunity to be together, away from a strict religious environment, and they had given both a chance to breathe fresh air.

Maxine's influence on her husband had been most positive during this period. Living with Maxine was teaching him about love, open-mindedness, and free-

dom. When she caught Jim smoking in the shed behind the house, she simply laughed, enabling him to
do the same. In his heart, Jim didn't feel such things
were important issues, but he couldn't step free from
the guilt of breaking the rules. He smoked his whole
life, but never felt the freedom to do it in public. In
essence, he feared the rejection and judgment of his
Christian peers.

In late September, 1936, Jim and Max pulled into
the Dallas Seminary campus. Maxine was there to be
with Jim; he was there to be with L. S. Chafer. Max
was excited at the prospect of having her husband
home at night.

While the men were in class, the wives had assorted
get-togethers. With little else to do, Max made these
meetings a regular part of her life. She recalls: "I remember a strong feeling that I didn't fit in. I'd look
around and see the conservative dresses, the ugly
shoes, and the missionary hairstyles—well, I didn't
like it at all, but I guess I felt they were right. I was
just a 'babe' in Christ, and many of these women were
long-time church members. After a while I started to
imitate them. I wasn't conscious of it at the time, but
in looking back I feel that I was losing my identity. I
was trying to emulate people that I didn't agree with
in my heart. I hadn't considered that the atmosphere
of a seminary just wasn't fertile soil for me."

Occasionally Max would go with Jim to his theology
class, taught by Chafer. She learned much from this
experience, but didn't know how to relate his input
with that of others. Many people at the seminary
talked far more about sin than about grace. Says Maxine: "I had never been exposed to people who talked
about sin all the time. I guess my concept of sin was
vastly different from theirs, but I had so little confidence in my own feelings. As I had done with Jim's
family, I figured that these people knew more than I,

so I was quite open to their teaching me what Christ was all about. So many things were considered evil that I just stopped living. That's when I started to wrestle with depression."

After the first year of studies, Jim committed himself to a summer job in Arizona. In her fourth month of pregnancy, Max was most reluctant to see him leave, but going with him was out of the question. Yet having had two miscarriages, she was most concerned that she might have a third. She had no desire to face it alone. Jobs were few and far between, however, and Jim felt he had no option; Maxine disagreed.

She had married Jim to be with him, believing that his only desire was to be with her, and she had no desire to face life's problems without her man close by her side. Ironically, Jim needed a strong woman who could keep the wagons rolling while he was up ahead scouting out the territory. After much debate, Jim headed for the country to lead summer youth camps, and Max stayed behind in the seminary apartment.

Several weeks later Max saw a Western Union delivery boy on campus and deeply sensed he had a message for her. She was right. A telegram informed her that Jim was in an Albuquerque hospital. His appendix had ruptured, gangrene had developed, and his life was hanging in the balance.

Under severe emotional stress, Max called her doctor. He made it clear that her odds of avoiding another miscarriage were fifty-fifty if she stayed put, but he gave her no chance of having the baby if she traveled. Max desperately wished to be with her dying husband, but she didn't want to lose their baby. There was no other solution, she finally reasoned, than to stay where she was and pray for Jim's recovery. But with her husband hanging to life by a thread, demons Anxiety and Despondency waged war on Maxine's spirit. She was gripped by fear: fear of losing her husband

and her baby, fear of having to face life by herself,
and fear of her deteriorating emotions.

Jim's condition was critical. He had developed peri-
tonitis, a fecal fistula, and abdominal gangrene. As
there were no antibiotics in those days, his recovery
was unlikely. The foul odor of gangrene permeated
his room. Eventually the hospital staff put Jim's bed in
the doorway with his head in the hall. They draped a
sheet from the top of the doorjamb down over his
chest to provide an odor barrier. For thirty-five days
he was in this condition. Quite against the odds, Jim
continued to improve; when Jim insisted that he must
return home, his doctors reluctantly gave him permission to take the train back to Dallas. Maxine was only
weeks away from delivering their first baby, and there
was no way he would stay away so long as he had the
strength to walk.

Maxine remembers his arrival: "I met him at the
train station, and I was so excited to have him back! I
wasn't prepared for the shock, however. It was a
walking corpse that stepped off the train. He had
jaundice, so his color was awful, and he had lost
about forty pounds. He was very thin, very weak, and
still had an awful open wound in his abdomen. For
several weeks I was pretty sure he wouldn't make it."

But before long, Jim was continuing his studies as
best he could. After class he was taken to the Baylor
Medical College to be on exhibit for the medical students. The doctors of Dallas and Albuquerque were all
amazed that he recovered; it was unheard of for a
person to develop gangrene in the abdomen and live
to tell about it. The doctors called it a miracle.

On October 17, 1937, Max gave birth to their first
child, Elna Ann. The parents were proud and the baby
was healthy, but just ten days after the birth of their
baby, Max suffered a devastating nervous breakdown.

"They kept you in the hospital for ten days back

39

then," Maxine recalls. "I remember coming home with the baby and feeling like something was wrong with me. Jim was studying, our baby was sleeping, and I was resting on the bed. It hit me that I had never been around a baby and didn't know how to care for one. Also, Jim's recovery had been slow, and I was still afraid his condition would worsen.

"But mainly, I felt the environment of seminary was gloomy, and I didn't want to be there any longer. I was overcome with fear and depression. It was far worse than I can describe, like an emotional black hole. Suddenly, something snapped and I started to weep uncontrollably. I had trouble breathing and was overcome with a feeling of utter panic. It was the worst experience I'd ever been through." Max didn't rally from the depression for eight weeks, and much of her refreshing personality had been buried. It was not to fully surface again in Jim's lifetime.

Years later, Maxine came to understand that the main cause of her breakdown was not her fears about Jim's questionable health, nor was it her feeling of inadequacy about motherhood. The primary cause was her loss of interest in life itself. Maxine explains: "There's a song that says, 'If you want joy, real joy, wonderful joy, let Jesus come into your heart.' As I viewed the world around me, I saw so very few people who had anything I'd call joy. Once in a while you'd see a person with a certain light in his eyes, and you knew that person had found something wonderful. Dr. Chafer was like that, and Jim was kind of like that, and there were a few others, but most of the people at seminary were singing about a joy I couldn't see they possessed. To me, it was like a big masquerade party; everybody wore a mask.

"I was so tired of fighting the current. I loved to dance but dancing was considered sinful, so I quit. I had always paid attention to my appearance, but

make-up and hemlines were such big issues that I
quit trying to look nice. I had always been a nonjudg-
mental type, but I found myself adopting the very
same attitudes that I rebelled so much against. That's
when my problem with weight began. Almost everything I was interested in was called a sin.

"Now I see that as I quit being myself, my depression grew in intensity. Jim's illness and my fears
about motherhood were real concerns, but just the
straws that broke the camel's back. The major problem was that I was losing touch with the real Maxine.
If only I had known that the only thing Christ desired
for me was the freedom to be myself."

Max, like countless other Christians, was being
weighed down by a false message that Christ never
taught. The gospel of Jesus Christ does not destroy
people. It is not an adherence to rigid codes of dress
and conduct. It is not a religious exercise involving a
set of rules and regulations. But from the time the
church began, Christians have misunderstood the gospel. Paul, writing to Christians in Galatia, referred to
"so-called 'Christians' there—false ones, really—who
came to spy on us and see what freedom we enjoyed
in Christ Jesus. . . . They tried to get us all tied up in
their rules, like slaves in chains. But we did not listen
to them for a single moment" (Gal. 2:4-5, *The Living
Bible*).

Jim was being led by the indwelling Spirit to understand these truths, but while he was learning about
God's infinite grace, Maxine was sinking into a dismal
abyss of religiosity emphasizing a rigid code of behavior. Having little confidence in her personal percep-
tions, Max shut the door of her heart and tried to accept the rules and regulations she'd been taught. In so
doing she buried her spirit, and depression pounced
upon her as an eagle does its prey.

Jim had no understanding of Maxine's emotional

41

condition. He was accustomed to conservative religious environments and found the seminary atmosphere quite liberal compared to his past. He was learning from Chafer about the Holy Spirit, and his head was swimming with exciting new truths. With the aid of the Spirit, those new insights would work their way from Jim's head to his heart. But while Jim's spiritual sensitivity was growing like a young bear cub, Maxine's had gone into hibernation, victimized by those who preached on a mystery they didn't understand.

FIVE

Young Life

DURING the 1938-39 school year, Jim decided to take a part-time job with a Gainesville, Texas, church. Jim was the assistant pastor in charge of youth work; Clyde Kennedy, a minister with progressive ideas, was his boss.

Together the two men hashed out a novel idea—that Jim would work with unchurched kids exclusively, instead of with those who already attended. Nothing suited Jim better than this approach. Experiences in the Southwest had taught him that most high-school kids avoid church if at all possible. Besides, Jim wasn't fond of titles such as "minister," "youth worker," or "pastor," and he loathed black robes, clerical collars, and religious garb.

Armed with a soft spot in his heart for kids, a burning love affair with God, and a salary of five dollars a week, Jim headed for the local high school. Little did anyone suspect how far-reaching his efforts would be.

Jim studied every available book on youth ministries, yet failed to run across anything with which he agreed. Further searching led to a lady who was also working with high-school students; she called her group the "Miracle Book Club." As the kids didn't seem to mind the name, Jim adopted it for his group too. At first, progress was slow and results were disappointing. Meeting once a week after school in an empty classroom, Jim managed to interest eleven kids. For a man who loved to think big, this was a major disappointment; his "Miracle Book Club" was working no miracle.

I didn't know how to run a club. I started having it in the afternoon, after school. I'd talked the school people into giving me a classroom. I started with three kids. One of them turned out to be a Christian, and the other two didn't turn out to be anything. They just faded out. I got it up as high as eleven that year, but I'm telling you, it was the saddest bunch of sacks you ever saw in your life.

If you want to really see a bunch of sad apples, just have a meeting for the kids who'll stay after school. I got the biggest selection of teachers' pets you ever saw, not a red corpuscle in the whole crowd. Everybody I wanted to reach was out on the football field, and everyplace else, right while we were having our club meeting. After nine months of that, I knew I had to try something else.

Jim was learning that a high school is a complex subculture of its own. A person who fails to understand that subculture will never enter it. Kids run in cliques, and cliques don't usually intermingle. There are kids who are popular and kids who aren't. Neither group thinks highly of the other. A typical high school contains twenty to thirty separate groupings of students: athletes, eggheads, socialites, dopers, the drama crowd, the motorcycle crowd, college prep students, vocational students, the hot-rod gang, the party crowd, upperclassmen, lowerclassmen, blacks, whites, Chicanos, and so on. A person who plans to work with high-school kids had better know which ones he seeks to befriend. It is most difficult to interest all students in the same activity.

Jim hadn't foreseen this problem and didn't know how to address it. Experimenting with various approaches led him to a simple conclusion: attract the student leaders and they bring others; fail to attract them and attendance falls like a rock.

In the years that followed, Jim was often criticized for pursuing student leaders at the expense of equally needy kids who were less popular. But in no way did Jim view his method as beyond reproach—he had simply found a solution that produced results beyond his wildest expectations, and he rode the wave. It was not his calling to solve the sociological problems of the American high schools. Sociological problems are spiritual problems anyway. Solve the spiritual problem and you solve them both. Jim wanted kids to listen to the message of Jesus Christ, and he accepted any method which produced that result.

In January of 1940, Jim changed the Miracle Book Club format. The hour was changed from after school to early evening. And as kids preferred out-of-school activities, the meetings were moved into the homes of various students.

Jim described the beginnings of his success with high-school students:

What a change! I started having lively meetings. Two

45

or three kids came out who were really sharp and could do something with the rest of the bunch. Their personal enthusiasm for the club got others to come, and it was wonderful. Right at the start the Lord got hold of two kids. One of them was Viddie Sewell. She was the very first youngster that was ever led to the Lord Jesus Christ in a club of mine. She was in with that little high-school society set, and she got those kids to come to club, she and a boy in the senior class.

We decided we'd have a prayer meeting, those two kids and me. In the pastor's study that Sunday night, we started to pray for the club. The pastor met with us. He was pushing on me all the time. He didn't care if I did any work around the church. He just wanted to see those kids reached for Christ. He said, "Don't monkey around with the people who come to church. I'll take care of them. You go on down to that high school." Boy, now just think of that. I wonder what would happen if there were more pastors like that, if there were some pastors in every town like that. That just said, "Boy, I'm not doing so bad with the people who are coming to church. The thing that's bothering me is all those people who don't come. Somebody go out and get them." That's what the church is all about, really.

You can't read the book of Acts, you can't read the New Testament, you can't read of the life and ministry of Jesus Christ, without coming to the conclusion that that's what the church is here for, to go after others. And why it's such a colossal flop is because it's so ingrown. Nobody hears the message except those who've always heard it, and they're not going to do anything about it, so nothing happens. This guy just kept pushing me and pushing me and pushing me, and out I went.

I don't even think the prayer meeting was my idea. We'd had twelve kids at our club meeting the night those two kids came through for the Lord, and we de-

46

cided to have this prayer meeting, and the next week we had twenty-three. And boy, we had another prayer meeting, a prayer meeting that wouldn't quit. And the next week we had thirty-two. In two weeks we went from twelve to thirty-two. And then we had another prayer meeting, and the school was really out then. The next night we met in the biggest home in the whole town, and we had fifty-one. And right at the end of the meeting, one of the toughest kids in the senior class got up and said, "Wait a minute, I wanted to tell you that I accepted Jesus Christ while Jim was talking." It was like a bomb dropped in the place. None of us had ever heard of anything like that. It was wonderful! One or two others who had gotten "waked up" joined the prayer meeting the next Sunday night, and from fifty-one we went to sixty-two, and from sixty-two to seventy-five. We had two meetings of seventy-five, and kept praying.

A beautiful little blond girl, the school beauty queen, came to know the Savior and joined in that prayer meeting. She had never been in a prayer meeting in her whole life. We were praying around in a circle, taking turns, and she heard us praying for Burr Nichols, the captain of the football team. As soon as we raised our heads up from prayer, this little blond girl piped up and said, "I'll get Burr." Just like that! That prayer was answered fast! She was going with him, and she said she'd have him at the next meeting.

We started the next meeting, and that night I'll never forget. It was crowded in that hall where we were meeting. It was a big front hall, but seventy-five people are a lot of people for a hall. They were sitting on the floor, and I was crammed up against the front door. I kept looking for this blond girl and Burr Nichols. They weren't there.

We went through the songs, and it was time for my message. I'd stalled as long as I could, and just as I

47

was getting up to speak, there came a clomp, clomp, clomp across the front porch. That door busted open behind me and here was this little blond cutie and Burr Nichols right behind her. She just pranced in and sat down in front of me. That was the only space on the whole floor. And there was Burr standing in front of that whole crowd; he turned around and sunk down beside her.

Well, I started in, and I was scared to death. I was just shaking in my boots. I gave the gospel the best I knew. Burr hadn't been at the beginning of the meeting, he hadn't heard any singing or anything, but something about it he liked. He came around afterwards and stuck out his big mitt, shook my hand and said, "Boy, Jim, I liked that. I'm coming back next week."

Next week we started off with the same situation—a big crowd jammed up against the front door, but Burr Nichols wasn't there. I went all the way through and came to the message time again. I saw the little blond girl in the audience and thought, "Oh, oh, they've had a divorce this week." But I was wrong.

Just as I started to speak, there came the awfulest clomp, clomp, clomp across the front porch. Burr opened the front door and came in like he owned the place. He walked past me and said, "Jim, I wouldn't have been so late, but I couldn't find some of these guys." And four teammates came trailing in behind him.

I found out that across the street from the high school a group of elderly women had been meeting for six years, every Monday morning, getting down on their knees in the living room of dear old Mrs. Frazier's. They prayed every Monday morning for six years, long before I ever heard of Gainesville, Texas, for the high-school kids across the street. I was there a year before I heard of that prayer meeting. I used to go

48

over there with those five or six old ladies and get
down on my knees with them after that club started to
roll. That was the thing the Lord used to start it.

Back in seminary, a group of kids going to school
there got interested in this club and started to pray.
They'd meet every Monday night and pray while I went
to the club meeting in Gainesville. They'd get down on
their knees and spend hours praying for that club meet-
ing. It's no wonder we had a revival in that school!

That's how Young Life started. I didn't have in my
mind to start anything, but that club went from 75 to
96, and then to 100, and then to 119, and 135, and the
week before finals there were 170 kids there.

Burr Nichols closed in with the Savior about the fifth
night he ever heard the gospel. That fall Burr went to
Dallas to spot players for the announcer at one of their
games. Riding back, they had a terrible accident and
Burr was killed. His folks wanted me to preach the fu-
neral. They said I was the only preacher Burr had ever
listened to.

Burr grew up on the wrong side of the tracks and
was a regular ruffian. All the Lord was waiting for
was somebody to get a little bit interested in Burr—a
little blond beauty queen and a little pip-squeak theo-
logical student. Burr was a precious soul for whom the
Lord died. This country is full of people like that. There
are thousands of people in this country that no Chris-
tian has ever said a kind word to. Most of the kids in
this nation are like that. A few million more of them
will graduate from high school this year. Just like Burr
Nichols, they never heard the story. And I can't stand
that.

In half a year, attendance at the Miracle Book Club
had increased more than ten times. Results like these
were unheard of in Christian circles; those who knew
of Jim's success with the high-school crowd were
awestruck. Many were asking, "How could any man

attract such numbers of kids to a meeting where the gospel was presented?" The question implies that the life of Jesus Christ isn't interesting, at least not to teens, but Jim couldn't imagine that anyone who knew the gospel would think it dull. He reasoned, therefore, that a person who thinks this way just doesn't know the story. Further, Jim had already learned that young people are the most open-minded people in the world. Kids do not bring a head full of staid religious ideas into a personal encounter with Christ. When Jim talked about his Lord, no open-minded person thought it dull.

To love-starved young people, Jim sought to be a friend. Kids listened to Jim when they wouldn't listen to others because they knew he cared about them. And once he had built a bridge of friendship, he was naturally anxious to share the source of his love. Jim figured it is best to love first and save the evangelizing for later. He called it "earning the right to be heard."

Jim and Max's second child, Mary Margaret, was born March 13, 1940, just as the Miracle Book Club was getting off the ground. Jim's diaries mix gratitude for a healthy wife and child with praise for increased attendance at club meetings. But Maxine was not doing well as the seminary days drew to a close. Things had not been the same since her breakdown. Depression and fear continued to dominate her emotions. She had some good days, however, and was quite productive when her "sun was shining." For instance, she arranged for Jim to have an office space in the basement of a dormitory; she raised the money, purchased the furniture, and did the decorating in what she called "Early Flea Market" style. All this had been a surprise for Jim. But generally there were few surprises.

Fueling her problems with depression, Max had

been suffering severe lower back pain since the latter half of 1938. It was diagnosed as a herniated lumbar disc, the result of an earlier automobile accident. Max had deteriorated. She no longer felt good physically or emotionally. The "Christian" religion she'd acquired was not much help. The more she tried to follow the various "Christian" codes in dress, appearance, vocabulary, and lifestyle, the worse she became. She could not save her soul by burying her spirit.

Jim and Maxine had much to learn about communication, for neither was able to understand what was happening to the other. Ironically, the man that God was using to reach young people with the life-giving message of Christ seldom conversed with his wife about the subject. One night he wrote in his journal: *It is a real rebuke to my own heart that I have not often talked to Maxine of the Lord's precious dealings in my own life. May the Lord become daily more precious to her in a life of complete yieldedness to his perfect will.* This prayer would be answered, but not in Jim's lifetime.

In the summer of 1940, following his graduation, Jim went all over south Texas setting up contacts for more high-school clubs. Under the new name of "Young Life Campaign" (borrowed from a group in England), he held tent meetings in Houston, Dallas, and Gainesville. These were evangelistic crusades complete with a choir, quartet, and preaching. There was even a children's meeting. Jim's journal records his progress in Dallas:

8/18: *We started Dallas YLC (Young Life Campaign) today—220 in afternoon and 350 at evening meeting. I've not been at my best today—probably due to physical condition, but the Lord has greatly blessed.*

8/19: *51 at the children's meeting—260 tonight.*

8/20: 105 at children's meeting—325 at YLC. Excellent! Great time in prayer, both early a.m. and late p.m.

8/21: Our smallest crowd of this campaign—about 200. Good interest however.

8/22: High-school night—about 400—the Spirit was present in great power. It is amazing to see what he can do with kids!

8/23: Big crowd tonight. Great time in prayer, early a.m.

8/24: Full tent tonight—great crowd—over 500 in spite of storm.

That summer Jim spoke to thirteen thousand people in his canvas church. Approximately one-third were of high-school age. From June through August, he led forty-two services in the tent, spoke four times over the radio, led eleven club meetings with the high-school crowd, spoke at six church services in various cities, led two kids' camps, took twenty-one trips, had fifteen get-togethers with interested adults, spent seven days building tents, spoke at Rotary and Kiwanis three times, and saw Max through her second nervous breakdown.

Despite Maxine's pressing needs, Jim's life had become a hectic series of clubs to lead, sermons to preach, tents to build, prayer meetings to attend, classes to teach, and many other functions. He was excited about his budding vineyard, deeply touched by the sense of God's Spirit upon him, and convinced that in the high-school crowd he had an audience that would listen. Bubbling over with enthusiasm, he tragically left Maxine behind. Not having found the relationship with Christ that Jim knew, she couldn't possibly understand his dedication.

As the 1940-41 school year began, Max and Jim had to vacate their apartment at school. On moving day, Jim spoke at the Dallas Seminary chapel. Dr. Chafer had asked him to present his work with the high-school crowd. The next day Jim started teaching a class about Young Life. As a result of his chapel talk, sixty-five fellows signed up.

Little did the men in Jim's class know how quickly he would have them at the front lines. Many had come to his class to gain insights they could use later, but Jim was a recruiter, and his enthusiasm was contagious. Within days, many of these men found themselves walking around a high-school campus in Houston, Dallas, or Gainesville, making friends of kids and promoting the new clubs.

But as the work continued to prosper, Jim's situation at home continued to decline. His 1940 journal records his success at work and his problems at home:

10/10: *Left early for Houston. Had a good contact at Addicks High School. Fine rally tonight. Made plans for six new clubs to start Thursday, one week from today. Maxine bad tonight.*

10/14: *Many contacts today. Good meeting in Gaines-ville but only sixty-five. Coleman began at St. Joe with twenty kids. Harry had twenty at Myra. Maxine's condition bad.*

10/18: *Around home after shopping with Maxine and Elna Ann. Maxine really bad tonight.*

10/27: *An excellent time with John E. Mitchell this a.m. Took little Ann with me today. Maxine not well.*

10/29: *Maxine very bad this a.m. so I called off everything and came home. Made an appointment with the doctor for tomorrow.*

10/30: *Took Maxine to the doctor (psychiatrist). He was frank to say there may be no easy or inexpensive way out for us.*

10/31: *I picked up a mob of roughnecks tonight out in Harrisburg—some of them said they would come to YL next week. God seemed to lead to these guys.*

11/1: *Maxine very bad.*

11/6: *Maxine's doctor is definite. She needs to go to hospital.*

11/7: *Excellent Houston trip. Little Ann went with me. Three of the guys I picked up last week came to club. They were interested, too. God is faithful.*

11/8: *Returned from Houston in a.m. Felt bum—severe migraine—relief with shot. Maxine bad.*

11/9: *Took Maxine to hospital this a.m. Hated to leave her out there. Left for Houston on 5:00 p.m. train.*

Ann was three years old, Mary Margaret eight months, when Max was hospitalized. When he could manage, Jim took Ann with him; when he couldn't, she stayed with friends in Gainesville. Mary Margaret (Sue) was cared for by Ted and Mary Lou Benson, one of the young couples at seminary who later joined Jim to develop Young Life.

Three weeks after entering the hospital, Max was released. Her condition was no different from before. Before Max's breakdown, few things had given Jim more pleasure than coming home to Max and his "cute girlies," but coming home was no longer joyful. As Jim recorded in his journal entry of December 8: *A bad day. All family feeling bad and Maxine apparently doing no good. He alone can solve our problem.*

In spite of increasing marital problems, Jim's efforts to reach high-school kids continued to produce a

healthy crop. Doors were opening on all sides. Supporters began pressuring him to incorporate his work,
largely as a means of giving donors a tax deduction.
Jim wasn't enthused about the idea, but later changed
his mind without giving it further thought. His heart
was in presenting Jesus Christ to the high-school
crowd; if incorporating would benefit the cause, Jim
would vote for it. On December 24, 1940, the Young
Life Campaign board of directors was formed. The initial group was composed of Dr. Chafer, Ted Benson,
John E. Mitchell, and Jim. Legal papers of incorpora-
tion were filed ten months later.

Jim was caught napping on this whole issue. At first,
the idea seemed heaven-sent, as he had three dedicated and gifted men with him to chart the course
ahead and help steer the ship. Jim failed to consider,
however, the long-range ramifications of incorporating. The question is whether the Christ teaching can
successfully be married to the "corporate way" (but
that's another book).

Early in 1941, Jim decided to have a mass Young
Life rally in downtown Dallas at the Baker Hotel. Several of the men assisting him were dubious about the
plan, but as usual, Jim's opinion prevailed. "This is a
Red Letter Day!" Jim wrote in his journal February 24,
1941. "Attendance at the Young Life mass meeting
was 2,000, and many were crowded out. Program superb—great spirit—especially among the men of the
school."

Because of results like this, Jim received speaking
requests from churches, high schools, Bible colleges,
and other groups both near and far. It was all he
could do to keep up with the demands of his hectic
schedule. In one thirty-four-day stretch in 1941, during a trip to the Midwest and East Coast, he spoke
seventy-nine times. Back in Texas, things continued to
boom, as his journal shows:

55

2/7: Very busy day. Mailed out 850 letters to mailing list, and 50 personal letters to various leaders. Really do not know how to tackle this stupendous job. Exhausted.

2/9: A great day in Tyler with fifty kids in a fair meeting tonight. A fine group of kids.

2/10: Club #37 was the best we have ever had and the best I was ever in. The Holy Spirit was manifestly present, and the whole program went over well with the kids.

2/23: Fifteen hundred at the Roofgarden Rally. The crowd not as big as last, but the program was snappier and went over with a "bang."

2/24: A marvelous crowd of nearly a thousand—filling the huge Rice Ball Room.

2/27: The San Antonio mass meeting was "beyond that which we ask or think"—a great time. Everyone happy about the whole thing. Took 11:00 p.m. train for home. Great response tonight.

3/3: A great meeting of #37 tonight. I figured the financial needs for the mass meeting today and I am $250.00 short. Committed it to Lord this afternoon.

3/4: A check from Orville Mitchell—postmarked yesterday 3 p.m.—amount was $250.00. Just wipes out our deficit. It is amazing to see how the Lord works.

3/7: A very profitable and busy day at the office. Nice evening at home with the girlies! They are so sweet!

Jim was a hard-driving man, frequently working to the point of exhaustion. His fledgling work with kids had hardly left the cradle stage before the demands of fund raising, mailing lists, newsletters, recruiting, training, teaching, and travel were placed upon him.

Maxine recalls: "It just killed me to see Jim push himself so hard. I figured I was going to lose him early, as I couldn't see how a person could drive himself like that and not have it catch up with him sooner or later. When I brought the subject up, Jim always said he would rather burn out than rust out. I never understood why one should have to do either.

"He definitely believed his steps were ordered of the Lord. Believing this with all his heart, he trusted that he wouldn't take a wrong step, that the Lord would keep him on the road he should travel. I wished, however, that I could wave a little magic wand and say, 'Relax, Relax.' I always wanted him to take it easier, to spend more time with his family. It hurt me to see him in a tied-up condition."

Jim lived his life at a very rapid pace, but he did something few Christians do—he bathed his every move in prayer. These excerpts from his 1941-1943 journals show the importance of prayer to his work:

Had the best time of prayer of my whole life tonight. Did not feel like praying but knew I needed to more than anything. Just took the Lord at his Word and went to him with everything. He gave me great peace. As I study this thing, I am convinced that times of unrest are always due to failure in prayer.

Busy day at office—then to train. Little Ann going with me. She went right to sleep as soon as we climbed in our upper berth. Was so weary I couldn't pray very well. Oh, that I might never have days too busy to pray.

Rose at 4:50 this a.m. and spent from then till 6:00 a.m. in prayer. Oh how I long to go on with HIM 100%, gaining strength, grace, and wisdom for whatever each day may bring.

57

*A wonderful hour of prayer this a.m. I have been con-
victed more and more about the many days that I do
not really have much time ALONE for prayer. May
Psalm 143:8 ["Let the morning bring me word of your
unfailing love, for I have put my trust in you. Show me
the way I should go, for to you I lift up my soul." New
International Version] become my constant experience.
My main objective for 1943, on this New Year's Eve, is
that it shall be a "prayer year"—more than ever before.*

*Wrote letters, studied, and prayed this a.m. after sleep-
ing late. Spoke this evening on "Life's Greatest Opportunity," using Luke 18:35-42. Small crowd but much
good accomplished by the Holy Spirit, I believe. I have
a deep and abiding feeling of his presence, a sense of
real yieldedness to him, dating from a special experience of surrender and dedication to the Eternal Light,
which I experienced Saturday night in my room. Oh
for words to express!*

*I pray for a sufficient measure of his grace to do what
is pleasing to him in the office and in all dealings with
the staff. Oh, Father, make us READY and WILLING to
have no other purpose than to exalt Christ.*

*All day in prayer—no doubt the greatest day I've ever
had.*

58

It was this daily, prayerful dedication of his life, energy, and talents that opened many doors. In his efforts to meet and befriend America's high-school kids,
Jim had no proven method on which he could rely. He
would simply hang around a high school, week after
week, until someone finally asked him, "What do you
do, Jim?" And he'd say, "I lead Young Life Clubs."

"Young Life Clubs?"

"Yeah. Haven't you ever heard of Young Life Clubs?"

"Well, no . . ."

"You've never heard of Young Life? Why, it's the greatest thing happening! And you thought you knew what was going on around here, didn't you?"

Of course they'd never heard of it. There weren't any clubs in their town. So he'd lead them on, "It's the greatest thing! In Tyler High School, a hundred kids come to Young Life every week! You don't know about it?" Then he'd set up a date with them.

"Tell you what . . . get your girls and meet me at the hotel Tuesday night. We'll have supper together and I'll tell you about it." Usually they showed up. The appeal was a winner with kids.

In a stroke of "luck," the type that comes through faith, Jim received several invitations to address a high-school assembly. One open door seemed to lead to another. In almost every high school where Jim spoke, his was voted by the students the year's number one student assembly.

He really wowed the kids. He'd tell jokes for the first half of his talk—corny as can be. "High school isn't so bad, it's just the 'principle' of the thing." Kids would cheer and whoop and howl and the principal would get a little uneasy. Then he'd go on about "that cross-eyed teacher they had to fire because she couldn't see eye-to-eye with the principal." And, "I was talking to the principal this morning and he told me he just had to do something about all this kissing going on right under his nose."

59

The kids went wild. They didn't know who Jim was, but they knew they liked him. Then he'd tell them he was surprised that most people don't know anything about the greatest story every told. "People have lots of funny ideas about Jesus Christ, but very few know much about him. Since you kids want to be intelligent, and want your lives to work right, you at least ought to check out what he said before you decide. Everybody deserves a fair trial." He challenged them; he dared them. "Don't be ignorant, don't turn thumbs down on the greatest proposition in the world until you've checked it out." Within days, many of the kids were actively involved in Jim's meetings.

In city after city, Jim's new club was catching on. The staff was small, and it was not uncommon for a staff man to lead five clubs in five different cities. People pushed themselves to keep pace with Jim. After a particularly heavy week of assemblies, Jim was heard to say, "One of the reasons I'm eager for heaven is to see if these things do any good. Why, I'm so tired, the seat of my pants is wiping out my footprints."

Young Life's original staff of five men, led by Jim, had moved west, south, and east from Gainesville and Dallas. The salary was one hundred dollars per month. There was about the whole venture a simplicity and directness. There were no benefits or future guarantees, just the present moment to be spent in Christ's service. Jim had stepped out in faith, placing his needs and the needs of his people in the care of Christ. He had entered into the fire of testing and purification; little did he know how those flames would soon be fanned. Attempts to destroy and discredit him were lurking around the bend.

SIX. Big Ideas

BLISTERING charges of undermining church youth work were hurled at Jim from several of the major denominations. A Dallas association of religious educators and ministers from some twenty-five Protestant churches published specific criticisms. Front-page headlines in one church publication condemned him as a "shameful sham." The story quoted church leaders saying that Young Life was "irreverent . . . definitely harmful to the minds of young people."

Criticism mounted from all sides. Jim Rayburn is taking kids away from church. The music sung at Young Life clubs is jazz. Emotionalism runs high. Rayburn's thinking faded into oblivion long ago. Young Life is communist, a cult, politically subversive. Sensationalism reigns supreme. Jim was found guilty without a trial.

The whole episode was most painful, but it served to convince Jim that, by and large, the organized church had more problems than the kids did. Jim was a church boy himself, his father an evangelist, and he felt as if his own family had stabbed him in the back.

"Jim didn't mean to be blasphemous or irreverent," Maxine says. "He just knew the church was a colossal failure. He didn't mean for individuals to take this personally. He wanted Christians to face the reality of the situation, to care about the fact that as an organization the church was boring people because Christ wasn't presented. Jim didn't have any axes to grind or any big reformation to start. He just longed to see all the people in the churches—big churches, little churches—aware of what was happening."

Jim knew that he shouldn't put new wine into old wineskins. The new wine, Jesus as experienced in the Spirit, tends to lose its character if poured back into the old, religious ways of thought and life. Time with Maxine in the Southwest had moved him further away from the religious ways of his past, and he had loosened up considerably. Going to Dallas for study, however, was a step back into the church world. Jim recruited leaders from the church or seminary, spoke at every church that asked him, and required church involvement from his staff and family. When the Dallas area churches launched their attack, it reawakened him to his spiritual senses. New expressions found their way into his vocabulary: "the powerless church," "insincere conversion," "dead Christian," and so on.

Jim did not want to fight the church or to take kids away from it; he simply wanted to present the life and message of Jesus Christ in the warmest, most exciting way possible. Most churches had quit being warm and exciting long before Jim came on the scene. Further, the kids Jim was attempting to reach were not church kids. But trouble began when the church kids discovered Jim. He was a breath of fresh air to most of them; many, preferring Jim's meetings to their weekly youth group, promptly dropped out of church.

A few of those who knew Jim recall their impressions:

I went to a camp for kids, and there I met the man who was to become the greatest single influence on my life, Jim Rayburn. He shared his life, gave to me of himself, and influenced me in a way no other human being has ever done.

The greatest man I ever met—my life has not been the same from the day he first spoke to me.

One of the most unassuming, revered leaders of this century. I shall always have a vivid recollection of Jim—one that I will never forget. It was the time I saw him at prayer. His ruddy, infinitely kind face was lifted up, its features sharply outlined in light and shadow, like a Rembrandt portrait. The cares and deep concern of a fully committed life were writ deep in lines and furrows that gave him a weather-beaten appearance. Jim's whole being was in that prayer. When he had finished, his thin, muscular body was leaning forward in vibrant self-offering. His face, radiant with love, continued to pray long after his lips had closed, as if what he had to say could no longer be put into words. What an ineffable experience his prayer was that evening! I shall always think of it when I remember Jim.

He gave so much of God's love to me, and so many others—I miss him terribly!

63

Jim had a quality in his life unlike anything I'd ever seen. I knew from the first time I met him that I wanted to find whatever it was that he had found.

A visionary, and a man with the faith to see those visions through.

There was something burning in him; you could see it in his eyes.

What was burning in Jim's eyes is that which burns in the eyes of all men and women who know the wonder of God's abiding presence. To be touched, filled, indwelt, or baptized by the Spirit of God is to have your eyes and heart touched by the Master. It is the doorway into the fourth dimension. Jim was not an organizer, but an agonizer, frequently spending more time in prayer than in the office. For to hold the living water in your hand and see your brother die of thirst because he will not drink, is to know Christ's sorrow. Christ wept over it, and those who really know him do the same.

Jim felt that the twentieth-century "Christian" church had a woeful shortage of agonizers. "Christian" organizations, though, are loaded to the brim with organizers: time-management specialists, fund raisers, public relations experts, business experts, administrative experts, every kind of expert. Jim had no desire to start another such organization. "I always feel a tinge of embarrassment," he'd say in that slow drawl, "when I'm introduced as the founder of this outfit (Young Life), 'cause I never had any idea I was founding anything. It seems to me that the founder of something ought to at least know he was founding somethin', and I never did."

By the mid forties, Jim was speaking at 150 high-school assemblies per year and leading three to four Young Life clubs. He traveled extensively to promote the work, see his staff, and run a summer camping program for high-school kids.

On October 31, 1945, Maxine gave birth to their third and last child, James C. Rayburn III (the author). Jim recorded in his journal a week later: *Maxine and my little son came home today. He is very cute, and sweet, and I am a very proud pop. I just can't believe what is happening at Riverside High School. . . .*

Jim was a father figure to a far wider group than his immediate family. He filled that role for some of his staff and no doubt hundreds of high-school kids as well. He divided his schedule as best he knew, but there wasn't enough time or energy to cover so many bases. With Maxine's health and emotions on the ebb, Jim tried his best to fill in the void. He wrote in his 1944 journal:

10/20: *Worked hard at office and then took Ann (age 7) to her school dinner and carnival tonight. It was a mob, but I so enjoy doing things with the kiddies.*

10/21: *Took the kids to the circus this afternoon. Enjoyed it greatly, but I am very weary. Have been extremely worn out lately, to the point of exhaustion. Fun to be with the "girlies."*

65

By 1946, the Young Life staff had grown to twenty men and women; they could be found in Tyler, Houston, Dallas, Memphis, Tulsa, Chicago, Seattle, Portland, Bellingham, Yakima, and Mexico. Most looked to Jim for their encouragement, help, training, and finances. Some looked to him for their purpose, finding their purpose in his.

If there's a good excuse for exhaustion, Jim had it. The demands of Young Life were pushing him to his limit, his wife's health was a constant concern, and he fought a constant war with his own health problems.

From 1940 through 1946, he had two major surgical procedures performed on his abdomen, a yearly operation on his nose, and an ongoing battle with intense migraine headaches which sapped him of strength. Intense pain that peaked gradually was often accompanied by nausea and malaise. Jim was neither a hypochondriac nor a complainer; he truly suffered with this problem. From the onset of the symptoms through the termination of the headache, he was usually laid up for forty-eight hours. Rarely do his diaries fail to record how many days since the last migraine. Each headache cost him two days of productivity, and he could count on three a month.

The strain of Maxine's deteriorating health contributed to the stress he felt. Jim simply had no place to escape life's pressures and problems. The more he sought refuge in his work, the worse the problems became at home. Maxine says, "Since age fourteen, I was very sensitive about being rejected or abandoned. I understood Jim's usual absence as a reflection of me—as if I had been abandoned again or wasn't wanted. I hadn't found Christ, peace, love, or joy in Christianity—I had no personal knowledge of the Holy Spirit—so I really didn't understand what was happening, spiritually, to Jim. At times I made things pretty rough on him. Not knowing the power available to me, I fought life's problems in my own strength—and lost."

Maxine's lower back problem worsened each time she gave birth. After my birth, it was necessary to hire help, as she could no longer bend, lift, or carry. Living with intense pain only weakened her emotions further.

Tired, burdened, and lonely, in the midst of a vicious attack by the church, his marriage suffering, the demands of his work pushing him to his limit, Jim's undying faith and God-given love for kids drove him on. While on a trip to Colorado Springs, October 16, 1944, he spoke to four thousand kids in one day. That night he wrote in his journal:

What a day! Five assemblies! Every one of them filled. I can never thank the Lord enough for his grace and power to make me acceptable to all these kids.

I cannot write tonight. Surely I have never been privileged to see anything like it. In one day's time—this great throng of young people. And the presence and power of the Lord, by the Holy Spirit, every moment of the way.

By his grace alone I was enabled to produce the best day's ministry of my life. Tonight I gave the most forceful Gospel message I have ever given. The response of these dear and precious kids was like nothing I have ever seen before. All the boys agree that this was our greatest day in Young Life work.

I know God hears and answers my prayers. Am filled with grateful praise. With all my heart I am dedicating myself anew to the proposition of being all out for him, all the time, with no other purpose for which I live.

And prayer gave Jim both a purpose and the strength to carry it out.

11/8: *This has been one of the truly great days of my life. Shortly after going to bed last night, about 1:00 a.m., I became very restless. Soon got up, read the Word, and prayed. The Lord met me in such a strange and warm way as I bared my heart before him until 5:00 a.m. Then up at 6:30 and out to pray with the men. Came right back here where I spent the whole morning and most of afternoon in prayer and study. Oh, the joy of realizing that he is right here!*

11/9: *Another unbelievable day. The Spirit is doing something to me that has never happened before—giving me a consuming desire to be absolutely sold out to*

*Jesus Christ and completely dead to self and all else
that the world holds. Spent all day in prayer and the
Word, alone! It seems that my heart is almost to break,
just to enter into the truth of all things in Jesus. Now it
is 1:30 a.m. I have lost much sleep this week and have
not experienced the least bit of weariness in my work.
The Lord Jesus is more precious to me than ever before.
I want to know what it means to suffer for Jesus' sake.
May the Lord Jesus, by his Spirit, deal with me until
truly Christ be formed in me.*

*12/18: Prayer this a.m. Then off for a busy day. At
nearly midnight had a time alone with the Lord in
prayer. He met me in a way that has seldom, if ever,
happened before. Was the greatest time of worship I
can remember. How sure I was that I could not in the
least be fooling Jesus by pretending to surrender. I offered myself completely to him, regardless—Col. 4:12.
Was flooded with unspeakable peace; God was with me
in a more intimate way than ever before, as if I had
entered another realm. My greatest desire was to worship and thank him, though much of the time I could
not express any thought in words. An undefinable, unspeakable experience. I hope and pray that memory
will serve me to recall whatever of this precious time
alone with God I need to remember in days ahead. Am
quite sure I have never gone through such a season of
testing, so this mercy and sovereign grace of my God
means more to me than I can express. I do not want
anything in my life that is not of the Lord Jesus.*

The faith of those who know this intimacy with
Christ is seldom understood by others. In Jim's case,
almost every idea the Spirit laid on his heart was con-
tested by those around him. Such was the case when
Jim first felt the need to purchase a summer resort for
kids. By 1945, he was actively looking for a campsite

in Colorado. As salaries were minimal for Young Life
staff, few could understand his conviction. Some
thought he was crazy. Where would the money come
from? Jim didn't have the answer, but he trusted God
to provide.

In the spring of 1946, Herb Taylor, president of the
Young Life board of directors, received a call from Jim
concerning a property known as Star Ranch, a beautiful facility just five miles south of Colorado Springs.
Together with his wife, Gloria, Mr. Taylor flew to Colorado, looked over the ranch, and gave a thousand-
dollar check as earnest money.

A board of directors meeting was hastily arranged to
discuss the purchase. Several expressed a fear that
Jim wanted the property for his own personal enjoy-
ment. Some felt that kids from other parts of the
country would have no interest in Colorado. Most
were afraid to take on such a financial burden. There
was not one vote besides Herb's and Jim's to continue
with the purchase.

Herb, a staunch believer in Jim's vision, left the
meeting, sold part of his stock in Club Aluminum, and
purchased Star Ranch himself. He leased the property
to Young Life for one dollar per year; later, he do-
nated it.

That some believed Jim's interest in a camping
property was simply selfish shows how little these
men understood what was happening in their midst.
They were in the company of a young David, and few
felt he should tackle Goliath-size projects.

In future years Jim would be drained of much energy by persistent struggles with a doubting staff and
board of directors. Jim knew the inner prompting of
the Spirit, but he had to carry a skeptical group of followers on his shoulders. Eventually his knees would
buckle under the load.

In January of 1947, Jim lost his closest friend, a man

69

who understood him and whose faith was Jim's inspiration—Sid Smith, from Winnipeg, Canada. In spiritual matters, Sid was Jim's big brother. He had understood the consuming fire within Jim as few others had. Perhaps no death affected Jim more. He recorded in his journal:

1/28: *A wonderful day in Winnipeg. Assemblies at Kelvin and St. James Collegiate were too good to be true. Five radio broadcasts. Young Life quartet was good, Orien Johnson excellent. Twenty below zero, but a larger crowd than last night. Great to be with Sid. He's great!*

1/29: *Don't see how the Lord can bless me so much in this work that's so dear to my heart. Very large crowd tonight. Good meeting at Rotary for lunch, very well received. Sid and I had another of those sweet, special, intimate times of fellowship such as I never have with anybody else but him. So thankful to God for a brother who understands me.*

1/31: Sid went home today. *It was quick and quiet at 5:00 p.m. He was taken away to meet the Savior he loved. Of all the sweet memories I shall carry through life, none will match those of this dearest friend God ever gave me. How Sid loved Jesus! He loved him because he knew him. Sid taught me of Jesus and his great love as no other person ever did. He taught me what friendship means. He was my dearest friend and I shall never forget him. He loved me—I wonder why it was so?*

Sid often told me so sincerely, "Jim, no matter what you ever do, I will love you. No matter what you say, I will stand by you." He meant it! What a guy! His last week on earth was the happiest week of my life. God's wonderful grace shining through Sid made it so. I want to love Christ like he did. Sid had such great love

70

for the Savior that he even loved little guys like me.
Like Jesus did!

Years later, Sid's family would donate their summer residence to Jim's Young Life work. Thousands of America's teenagers would spend the best week of their lives at the Castaway Club in Detroit Lakes, Minnesota. This beautiful facility is a unique memorial to the special love shared by two of Christ's disciples.

Shortly after Sid's death, Jim and Max uprooted their three young Texans and moved to Star Ranch; they joined Charlie and Harriet Johnson, who had already settled in with their three young children. Jim commuted between Dallas and Colorado Springs for several months. Then the entire headquarters was moved into a log cabin in the woods.

Jim's adversary was close behind.

SEVEN

Two Ranches

MOST American teenagers consider Christians dull. A vast majority of adults share this viewpoint that sees Christ as for old people, boring people, sick people, or dead people. This tragic misconception, this ultimate lie, burdened Jim's heart. He knew: *Christ is life.* Without the intimate relationship with God's abiding Spirit, a person is dead (Matt. 8:22). To know Christ personally, through the Spirit, is to be born into true life, the realm above the senses. It is the pinnacle of human experience.

Jim's resorts for kids gave him an opportunity to demonstrate his concept of life in Christ. A week with

Jim and his crazy, talented followers was akin to a
week on Fantasy Island. He did everything with a
verve and zest that showed his love of life. It was contagious, this constant urge to stretch every nerve and
muscle, to go beyond the mundane patterns of life,
and Jim's growing staff caught his spirit of adventure.

Although few had shared his vision of a camp in the
Rocky Mountains, all were ecstatic when it material-
ized. Jim's staff bought bunk beds, repaired and
painted old furniture left at the ranch, and cleared
ground for a baseball diamond and volleyball court.
Everyone felt the spirit of excitement. A staff member
remembers: "It was so beautiful we'd sleep outside in
the summer. We were so excited we'd get up at four
o'clock in the morning. We found some old horse
blankets and I remember washing those by hand. You
see, the ranch was ours, and we felt it. It was part and
parcel of us. Our blood was in it."

The key to running a successful camp was quality.
In a time when lean-tos, tent houses, and meager surroundings were synonymous with Christian camps,
Jim insisted on excellence. He'd say, "Who started the
idea that Christians ought to have the seat of their
pants in patches, or that we ought to have camps in
tents? We talk about the King of Kings; let's act like
he's the one in charge! We're gonna get the classiest
camps in the country."

Jim had made a club leader of Orv Mitchell, a
prominent Dallas businessman. Orv was the first to
accompany a trainload of Texas kids to a Christmas
camp where Jim was to speak. As they pulled into the
train station at 5:30 in the morning, the Young Life
brass band greeted them with a blasting reception;
then a caravan of cars, overflowing with noisy, excited
kids, wound south toward Star Ranch. At the darkest
part of the road the caravan was stopped by a tall

masked bandit (John Miller) who threatened to re-
lieve everyone of their spending money. Orv's son Bob
was driving the first car, and much to the horror of
the kids, Bob took a very large pistol out of the glove
compartment. With one left-handed shot, he dropped
the bandit into a ditch and drove off. Within minutes
of their arrival, the kids had received a noisy, enthusiastic welcome, been held up, and seen a gun fight.
And they hadn't even reached the gate; it wasn't yet
time for breakfast!

After several days of high adventures, many laughs,
good food, and thoughtful consideration of Jim's mes-
sages, the kids headed home. Some left with a new
song in their heart, a new understanding of Christ.
But everyone left knowing they'd experienced something special. That brief exposure to a gracious host
and a loving atmosphere melted many false impressions of Christ.

Star Ranch did more than provide a resort for high-
school kids; it served as a center for bringing people
together. Jim enjoyed having a showplace where he
could welcome adults and share his vision. Several
Colorado Springs couples caught that vision and gave
generously of their time and money: Gus and Mildred
Hill, Howard and Emma Hanson, Ross and Elsie Lane,
Harold and Anita Brubaker, Kermit and Lorene Brubaker, Joe and Lucy Hatton, Jack and Edith Benson,
and Bob and May Parker. These folks were instru-
mental in giving Jim's young mission a foothold in
Colorado.

Moving to the ranch provided Jim more time with
Maxine, more time for his children, extended exposure to the high-school kids he loved, and a quiet forest in which to seek his Father's guiding hand. But by
1947 Maxine's back problem had become acute, and
the situation was affecting the whole family. In Febru-

75

ary of 1948, corrective surgery was attempted. Jim wrote: *Maxine in surgery this a.m. She has extreme postoperative pain, but they are keeping her sedated and she sleeps most of the time. Thank God it is over with!*

Jim was flooded with relief; for the first time in years there was light at the end of the tunnel. It looked as if the long, strenuous ordeal was over; there were better days ahead. But coming weeks proved that the attempt to fuse bone chips into the herniated spinal disk had failed. If anything, Maxine's pain was more intense than before surgery.

The operation's failure launched our family into a new era of darkness. We were standing on the precipice of a bad dream. Maxine recalls: "I was most naive about drugs; it had never even occurred to me to ask for a painkiller. But after the surgery I was given a large supply of Seconal to help me sleep. Soon I was reaching for a pill every time I felt pain, discouragement, or depression. It wasn't long before I was hooked. I had no idea of the devastation this would cause my family. By the time I recognized my dependence on these drugs, it was too late to stop. I felt I couldn't face life without them."

The nightmare had begun. Before it ran its course it would discredit Jim as a husband, discredit Maxine as a wife, fragment the family, and carry Max to the outer limits of loneliness and suffering.

Shortly after Max returned from the hospital, Jim almost lost his beloved ranch. As if an adversary was attempting to destroy his work, a fire of undetermined origin broke out near the offices. Star Ranch was nestled up against the mountains in a rather dense forest and was most susceptible to fire. Fanned by high winds, the fire spread rapidly and threatened to destroy the entire ranch. As the flames were about to

jump the last barrier, a providential change in wind
direction kept the fire from spreading further. A
spring snowstorm quickly moved in and extinguished
the threat; God's hand had spared the ranch. But the
fire had done little to help Maxine's nervous frame of
mind.

Several months later, on a slow, peaceful, summer
afternoon, an earsplitting clap of thunder rumbled
through the ranch. As the shock wave rolled by,
everyone snapped to attention, momentarily stunned.
The ensuing silence was interrupted by a young child's
shriek, "A big spark hit my daddy, a big spark . . . !"
Sue Rayburn, age eight, had been an eyewitness.

Jim, Bud Carpenter, and Tom Henderson, a young
camper, had all been struck by a vicious bolt of lightning. All three were down; none was conscious. As
some staff members ran to a telephone, others quickly
carried the comatose bodies to a nearby cabin. Maxine recalls:

"I never heard a deeper, louder clap of thunder; it
really jolted me. I can't explain it very well, but I
knew something was wrong; somebody was hurt. As
fast as I could manage with the big metal back brace,
I headed out the door and followed everybody else. I
had already learned that Jim was hit by the time I
reached the cabin. Through the door I could see the
doctor working feverishly. Then someone hustled me
away and accompanied me back to the house. Before
long a strange man knocked on the door and asked to
use the phone. I asked him who he was and he replied, 'I'm the county coroner.' "

Tom Henderson, a young man attending Young Life
camp for the first time, had been killed instantly. Bud
Carpenter, one of Jim's dedicated early followers and
a long-time staff man, was the first to regain consciousness. Jim, jolted to within an inch of his life,

had burns on his shoulders and intense pain in his head and legs. He was lucky to be alive. The lightning bolt, however, produced the longest interval in Jim's life without a migraine headache—five months. Jim wrote in his 1948 journal:

8/24: *About 5:00 p.m., as we were leaving the ball field, lightning struck, killed Tom Henderson and knocked out Bud and me. I awoke in the "Squirrel House" shortly before Dr. Karabin came. Have terrible pain in head and legs. Feel most peculiar. Am thankful to the Lord for sparing me, but can't help thinking a lot about him leaving me here when Tom was so very young.*

8/25: *In bed all day. Pain receding in a.m. Comfortable by evening. Maxine's condition set back badly by this shock. We are naturally upset by this young man's death.*

8/26: *Able to get up today. Conducted a short service this evening. Maxine's state of mind very bad; her nerves are shot. Left 10:30 p.m. for plane to Chicago.*

Within a six-month period, Jim had lost his wife to drugs, nearly lost his ranch, and barely survived a bolt of lightning. Fires and lightning would not keep Jim on the canvas, but the increasing weight of Maxine's illness was beginning to wear him down. By 1949 the stress was apparent. Jim's journal tells the story:

5/18: *Didn't go to Pueblo for club tonight on account of Maxine's condition.*

5/30: *Very tough migraine began in afternoon, lasted all night. Maxine sick all day.*

5/31: *Up at 5:30 in spite of sleepless night. Pain finally gone. Climbed up Cheyenne Mountain to Strawberry*

Point for prayers and breakfast. Came home to busy day in office. Maxine sick and distraught.

10/8: *A wonderful morning of prayer with the staff at headquarters. A hard afternoon—Maxine sick.*

10/9: *A wonderful class at church. A large crowd that was very attentive. Maxine very ill, spent rest of day with her. Feel very poor.*

10/19: *Up all night with Ann. She had another bad asthma attack. Feel very beat up this morning. The health problems of family, weariness, and almost daily conflict with pain in my head is making serious inroads into my health and life. Good club in Pueblo tonight—I took the girls.*

In spite of family problems and the pressures of leading a rapidly growing work, Jim's rapport with kids was keener than ever. His 1948-49 journals show this side of the story too.

4/23: *Spoke at Queen Ann's High. Have spoken to nine thousand kids this week, with great reception. Cannot thank the Lord enough.*

10/18: *Sick all night with migraine. Grand club meeting tonight, but more kids than we could possibly handle.*

10/26: *187 at the Colorado Springs Club, average attendance for the fall is 170 per week. Only two hecklers—the rest were very attentive. These dear kids will never find out how wonderful Christ is until they have faith. Oh, that I can produce a little seed!*

4/5: *A good club tonight with eighty-four kids—spoke on Luke 23.*

9/28: *Grand club in Pueblo tonight. Hard to believe how God is blessing this work.*

*10/3: A great high-school assembly for me in Yuma,
Colorado. A wonderful reception from kids and faculty.
Started club there tonight with sixty kids. Drove home
after meeting. A great 22-hour day.*

Jim was a master at handling the high-school
crowd. Kids tried everything imaginable to upset him,
tease him, or gain the upper hand, usually to no avail.
After one Young Life club in Texas, he found his car
had been carried up some stairs and deposited on a
stranger's porch. That Jim took such things in stride
only increased his rapport with the pranksters. Their
efforts to frustrate him were successful on occasion,
but he never let them know. On October 12, 1949, he
wrote: *Some tough kids tonight! A rather discouraging
club. I tried to speak on John 2, but never got to the
actual miracle.*

A reformed heckler remembers: "At one club a
friend and I were cutting up. During the singing we
were tossing song books down on the head of another
fellow. Finally Jim said, 'Sam, you're too noisy. Come
down here and sit.' He indicated the front row among
all the ninth-grade girls, and I was a junior. I was
mad, yet I had so much respect for Jim that I went
and sat there. I fumed; I glared; I stared at him. All I
wanted was to get even and upset him. He continued
club unruffled. He talked this time about successes in
sports and popularity, how one could have all the
things he wanted in high school, and still not have
real life—contentment, joy, peace inside. Because I
was so intent on trying to frustrate him, I actually
heard what he was saying. 'The only way to know
what real life has to offer is to know Jesus Christ.' I
kept listening. He quoted 1 John 5:12: 'Whoever has
God's Son has life; whoever does not have his Son,
does not have life' (TLB). This really hit me, and I
started thinking and evaluating what was going on in

my own life. Many years later, here I am actively leading a Young Life club and a college leadership group.
It's the closest thing to New Testament Christianity
that I know of."

Other former roughnecks recall their impressions:

> "I never saw anything that quite satisfied me until
> I saw Young Life . . . and I'd have to say until I met
> Jim. I was impressed with the club, but it was
> Jim's vision and compassion that impressed me
> most."

> "I'd grown up in church and thought I understood
> what Christ was all about. Then I met Jim Ray-
> burn. I felt I could listen to him talk forever. He
> was funny, honest, and genuine—not at all what I
> was used to. Jim led me to an encounter with the
> Spirit of the risen Christ. Now I know the secret
> behind the man."

> "I was never afraid to take my friends to Young
> Life. I knew they weren't interested in Christ, or
> anything related, but I also knew they had never
> met Jim. He was great; probably the best thing
> that ever happened in our high school was Jim's
> club."

81

Many have said, in jest, that they had their first
spiritual encounter while hanging from Jim's moun-
tain-climbing rope. There you'd be, clinging to a tiny
spur of rock, your feet barely riding a narrow ledge,
the wind threatening to blow you off the face of the
cliff, and Rayburn would shout down, "Isn't this the
most gorgeous place you've ever seen?" Once, in just
such a situation with his daughter Ann, he shouted,
"Smile, honey, I want to take some good pictures." Jim
was like that. He loved life and believed God wanted
us to experience it fully. His life was one of high ad-

venture, and it would be impossible to separate the man from his mountains. When Jim needed to go to "church," when he needed to find his Savior's hand, he headed for the high country.

By the summer of 1949, the third season of operation at Star Ranch, Jim was secretly shopping for a second resort. His search for the right property took him west to Buena Vista, Colorado, where he had spent many summers as a young boy. Together with Gus Hill, a close friend who shared Jim's concern for kids, he struck gold.

Byrd Raikes Fuqua, a visionary lady cut from the same cloth as Jim, had built what many considered the finest vacation resorts of their type in the country. The Byrd Colonies, as she named them, were composed of three units: Radio Spring Byrd Bath, the Alpine Lodge for Boys, and the Tin Cup Dude Ranch. Each unit was separate from the others, but all three were located in the heart of one of the most scenic spots in the State of Colorado. The great continental divide of mountains, the climate, and the general surroundings equal or surpass anything to be found in the Alps or elsewhere in the United States.

Old age and deteriorating health had forced Byrd Fuqua to sell her interest in these resorts. Upon transfer of ownership, the Radio Spring Byrd Bath became known as Chalk Cliff Lodge. Within the property boundary were the Hortense Hot Springs, the hottest in the state, having a temperature of 187°F at the point of issue. Byrd, who had lost her sight during World War I years, claimed that bathing in these hot waters had restored her vision. Whatever the medicinal effects, these natural hot springs were of keen interest to Jim, who had bathed in these waters as a young boy. By the summer of 1949, Chalk Cliff Lodge was once again for sale; Jim was back on his knees asking God for the property. Wally Howard, one of the original team, recalls:

"His faith had a daredevil quality about it. There were times when I could not decide if he was a man of God or just presumptuous, whether he was driven by ambition to serve Christ or to build his own empire. I wrestled with that, and I actually did not know. Sometimes I was angry because I thought him on an ego trip; then I would be humbled by the quantity and persistence of his faith, even after I questioned it."

Jim knew his interest in acquiring Chalk Cliff Lodge would be viewed as another irresponsible idea. Although he was reluctant to seek approval from his board of directors, God had laid it on his heart and he had to face the music. In September of 1949, he and Max went to Chicago to see H. J. Taylor. Jim's journal tells what happened.

9/25: *Fourth day in Chicago and I haven't done what I came here to do. Am very reluctant to do what I know I should—go see Mr. Taylor and Mr. Crowell about Chalk Cliff. Spoke at La Salle Bible Church this a.m. Maxine and I just loafed rest of day.*

9/26: *Felt very "backwards" this a.m. about doing what I knew I had to do. Finally went to meet with Mr. Taylor and Mr. Crowell. The Lord rewarded me greatly. A most refreshing time with both men. Feel relieved—a restful afternoon on the train with Maxine.*

9/27: *175 at my club tonight at ranch. A hard-to-handle crowd but went well. This is the end of a perfect trip. Maxine and I were greatly blessed in Chicago, especially yesterday. Thanks be to God!*

11/17: *A very hard day. In the midst of extreme pressure regarding the Chalk Cliff Lodge affair. Have to contact more board men! Feel discouraged and disillu-*

83

sioned. Oh, Father, have I misjudged your leading? Severe migraine—just about on ropes!

11/18: *A day of prayer—was difficult for me—extreme pressure—felt bum. Then the letter arrived announcing the marvelous gift from the Crowell Fund for purchase of Chalk Cliff Lodge. Am speechless! Thank the Lord! His lovingkindness is everlasting (Psalm 136)!*

One month and several miracles later, Young Life took possession of Chalk Cliff Lodge. The name was first changed to Star Lodge, then later to Silver Cliff Ranch. The first kids' camp there was held during Christmas vacation, 1949. Since then, over a hundred thousand high-school kids from every region on the globe have been guests at this beautiful resort.

Silver Cliff Ranch, like Star Ranch, was obtained by virtue of Jim's faith in God's ability to do what man cannot do. God is a rewarder of those who seek him; Jim was a tenacious seeker. God did not bless Jim's efforts because he walked in love at all times or because he was a faultless leader. God answered Jim's prayers because Jim believed in his heart that God is faithful, and that God had spoken to him through the Spirit. A man's faith is reckoned as righteousness (Rom. 4:5).

84 The beautiful Silver Cliff Ranch stands today as a memorial to a man who wouldn't limit God's willingness and ability to overcome obstacles. It stands as a silent lesson to those who thought it nothing more than a crazy dream concocted by an irresponsible dreamer.

Star Ranch was sold by the Young Life Campaign, Incorporated, in 1972. As this book goes to press, the Silver Cliff Ranch is being sold as well. Once kids had to be turned away; there weren't enough beds to hold them. Today the eerie silence of empty cabins seems to mourn the death of a dreamer.

EIGHT

Attack

IN 1950, Maxine was hospitalized once again
for further treatment on her back. Early in the morning, January 17, a nurse charged into her room and
removed the radio. Maxine recalls:

"I thought, 'Now that's a funny thing. Why would
anyone want to take away the radio?' I knew something was wrong, something had happened. About that
time a cleaning person came in the room and made a
remark about the terrible fire on Cheyenne Mountain.
I demanded the radio back. Eventually they returned
it to me. The first thing I heard was a report from
people close to the scene, broadcasting from a mobile

unit. The reporter said that Star Ranch was surrounded by fire and that all the people at the ranch were trapped. I'm not sure what I had in mind, but I went straight to the nurses' station and demanded to be taken as close to the ranch as possible. I was escorted back to my room, and in no time at all another nurse appeared with a hypodermic needle."

Seemingly every man, woman, and child who could walk, including one youth with his leg in a cast, offered to aid the regular fire-fighting agencies. The Colorado National Guard, Seabees, Soil Conservation Service, Naval Reserve, Forest Service, and many other organizations were on the scene.

By 5:00 a.m. volunteers were flocking into police headquarters. Colorado College men turned out in a body and were scattered throughout the fire area by those in charge. At Camp Carson, the large army base, every available soldier was called out. Fire-fighting equipment from Colorado Springs, the Broadmoor, Camp Carson, El Paso County, and Pueblo aided in battling the flames. Calls from fire departments offering equipment and personnel were received from all over the eastern part of the state.

Throngs of volunteers who came to police headquarters were hauled to the area in Army buses, dump trucks, police cars, the paddy wagon, and moving vans from the Weicker Transfer and Storage Company. Officer Tom Hughes, who was hauling people to the fire in the police paddy wagon, said the wind was so strong he feared the vehicle would be blown over on its side.

Those of us who were living at the ranch will never forget this nightmare. Says Harriet Johnson:

"Somebody, we never found out who, called us about 4:00 a.m. and asked if we knew of the fire. I said, 'No, where?' They said it was moving fast, and that it was headed in our direction. While I dressed our children, Charlie ran up to tell Jim. Shortly after he returned, we loaded the kids in the car and took off. We were sure Jim was right behind us.

"Half a mile from the ranch, the quantity of smoke crossing the road made it difficult to see. We turned on the lights, started honking the horn, and tried to continue. Twice we ran off the road, and at one point we were driving through tongues of flame. Eventually we made it out and pulled off the road to wait for those behind us. We waited and waited, but nobody came. We were sure that the boys in the jeep, and Jim and his children, were trapped, possibly burned. It scared me to death, thinking about that."

I was four years old, but the memory of that inferno will live with me forever. My sister Ann, age thirteen at the time, has a vivid recollection: "I'd heard the phone ring in the middle of the night, and I heard Daddy say, 'Oh, no!' Then he came to my room, shook me, making certain I was awake, and told me there was a big fire on the mountain. He asked me not to worry, to wake up Sue and Jim III, help them dress, and wait in the living room for him to return—that he needed to leave and see what the situation was. He said, 'I'll be back, so please don't worry. You know I wouldn't leave you here. You must stay here where I can find you, no matter how frightened you are; you must not run.' Then he left, and the three of us huddled together in the living room. We could smell the smoke, and we were scared.

"Soon Daddy came running in the door and said it was time to leave. He was visibly shaken, and just ran us to the car. Once outside, we kids were startled. The sky was bright red! And the wind was unbelievable; it was difficult to breathe. Pine trees were exploding all around us, sending flames hundreds of feet into the sky. I kept thinking, 'I just don't believe this, I can't believe this.' It was horrifying. Daddy let it get close before he gave up saving the ranch, deciding instead to get us out of there.

"The trip down the road was wild! Daddy said to roll up the windows as we were going to make a run for it, and that's exactly what we did. We literally drove through a tunnel of flame. What a ride! At times, the flames would jump across the road and we had to drive through them. Stopping would have been suicide.

"As soon as we were off the mountain, Daddy left us at a friend's house and headed back to fight the fire. He was determined to save Star Ranch, I guess. I begged him not to return, but he loved the ranch, had sacrificed much to get it, and couldn't be stopped."

A city utilities crew had first noticed the fire at 1:00 a.m. just to the south of the Broadmoor Hotel's new golf course. Workmen had been burning brush cleared from the area the day before. A sixty-mile-an-hour wind arose in the night, fanned the embers into flames, and blew them into dry scrub oak bushes surrounding the clearing. The gale-whipped flames spread rapidly to the southeast toward Camp Carson, south toward Star Ranch, and southwest, taking the fire up the face of Cheyenne Mountain. By 4:30 a.m. it had reached Star Ranch, having already burned thousands of acres. By noon it had climbed Cheyenne Mountain and destroyed the Colorado State Patrol radio broadcasting tower, interrupting communication with their patrol cars.

At one point, the flames, now whipped by hurricane-force winds, had surrounded Star Ranch and were threatening to close the circle. Gus Hill recalls:

"Our backs were to the walls of several buildings at the ranch. The flames had gotten so close! It was difficult to breathe, due to the smoke and gale-like winds. The only thing we could do in the strongest gusts was cover our faces and lie on the ground. Burning pine needles would blow into the side of a building and penetrate enough to stick. It looked as if the whole ranch would burn. At one point, I heard a bulldozer coming in the back gate. As I looked up, the wind blew the driver out of the seat and rolled him off the side."

By late afternoon, it was apparent that the ranch had been spared. One cabin and the corral tack room had burned to the ground; one large dormitory lost its roof; but the rest of the buildings were intact, even though burning mattresses were pulled from some of them.

Two major fires within a twenty-one-month span had failed to claim the ranch. Against the odds, Star Ranch was standing, ready to host another group of kids that following summer. It had been a very close call, however.

It seemed fortunate that Maxine was not at home the morning of the fire. The event was altogether too traumatic for anyone with a serious nervous condition. But hearing that her family was trapped was a traumatic experience in its own right, perhaps worse than being at the ranch.

Jim had no idea how to help Maxine. Hers was a tangled web of physical, spiritual, and emotional problems which had baffled many a doctor and psychiatrist. There were no simple answers. Jim tried to do the right thing for her, but things backfired in his face repeatedly.

89

After the 1948 forest fire, he took Max on a mini-vacation to help calm her nerves. Together they selected a quiet little town on the western slopes of Colorado, Glenwood Springs. They figured it would be a nice, peaceful place to spend a few days together, away from any problem or tension. Jim wrote:

5/9: *Maxine and I left at 3:00 p.m. for Glenwood Springs after much hasty office work. We had a superb trip through my favorite part of the mountains and ar-*

*rived at the Hotel Colorado at 9:30 p.m. where we
quickly bedded down in a nice big room.*

*5/10: Slept late this morning. Had a delicious breakfast
with Maxine, and then I fooled around town getting
car serviced. We went to Aspen for lunch. I was greatly
impressed by the chair lift. Then we drove back to Bas-
alt and went up the "Frying Pan" where Maxine
camped as a child. Then on to Redstone and Crystal
Rivers Lodge. Came back to hotel at 6:30 p.m. for dinner at 8:00. Really a grand day!*

*5/11: Wonderful day with Maxine in Glenwood
Springs.*

On the 13th, Jim had to leave for Chicago. The vacation had been so peaceful, Maxine decided to stay
in Glenwood for a few more days. She remembers:
"The day after Jim left, I decided to walk to the dime
store to buy some material; I wanted to make some
doll clothes for the girls. It was a peaceful, relaxing
day, and I was feeling better than I'd felt in years.
Pretty soon I heard a siren. People were scurrying
around like ants. I walked across the bridge to the hotel without much concern, but when I arrived, I
learned that the fire was in the oil and gasoline storage area just three or four blocks away.

90

"After the Star Ranch fire, I was a nervous wreck.
And by the time I got back to the hotel in Glenwood I
was pretty shook up again, so I asked a couple across
the street if I could stay with them awhile. They noticed how frightened I was, so she went inside and got
me a glass of sherry.

"Then it happened. The first of several tanks blew
up. It was a sound like I've never heard before. There
was a bright flash, an incredible boom, and a huge,
billowing, mushroom-shaped cloud of black smoke
and flame. We were almost blown over by the shock
wave and intense heat. Then tank number two, fifty

thousand gallons of gasoline, went flash-boom! The sky appeared to be on fire; it was like the town was being bombed. There were six or seven storage tanks, and they started going off one right after the other. People were screaming, and we were all crawling around on the ground trying to protect ourselves. It was horrifying!"

There hadn't been a day like that in Glenwood Springs before, and there hasn't been one since. Was Max simply in the wrong place at the wrong time? A sinister pattern of traumas had seemed to follow Jim and her ever since their marriage. It seemed that someone, somewhere, was bent on their destruction. For now, the attack was focused on Maxine.

Max was an enigma. She was sensitive to other people's problems, curious about the world she lived in, extremely perceptive, and fun to be with, but her delightful personality would come and go like the tides. When inspired, she could cook like Julia Child, paint like Van Gogh, and write like Kahlil Gibran. But this free-spirited personality was locked into a deep inner conflict.

When the tide was out, Max was an altogether different person. After any trauma she slipped further and further away from her true self, becoming withdrawn, depressed, pessimistic, scared of her own shadow, irritable, and prone to heavy drug abuse.

91

By 1950 her nervous state and deepening drug dependency were out of control. In a desperate search for help, Jim took her to the Johns Hopkins University Clinic in Baltimore, Maryland, believed by many at the time to be the best facility available for treating those with drug dependencies.

The people at Johns Hopkins offered no solution to Maxine's problem. Their chief contribution was in verifying that the spinal surgery of 1948 had failed to provide her with any relief.

Jim never stopped trying to introduce his lifestyle to

Maxine, in hopes that it would do for her what it had done for many others. He and his followers had no time for depression in their constant quest to see new places, meet new people, and do new things. But few things met with more failure than his frequent attempts to get Max off the sickbed by introducing her to his life of high adventure.

A case in point was the October, 1950, family vacation to Alaska. Dr. McClellan, a missionary doctor who had converted a World War II naval minesweeper into a hospital ship for visits to the remote coastal hamlets of the last American frontier, had invited Jim to join him on a trip from Ketchikan to Sitka, with stopovers at such "famous" ports as Hydaburg and Klawock. The plan appealed to Jim as if he'd dreamed it up himself; he was excited to be taking his family. Maxine recalls:

"The people on the ship were very nice, and they did their best to make that old minesweeper as comfortable as possible. The doctor, who was also the captain, had a radio on board, which gave me some comfort, but my impression was that no one really knew much about boating. They were just boat-happy people having a good time and providing a much needed service.

"The whole thing scared me; our kids, especially Jim III, were so young. I was scared to have the children running around on deck, so I made Jim III wear a life jacket at all times. Ann and Sue had to sleep at the other end of the boat, and I wasn't comfortable with that at all. Had there been an accident or fire, I was too far from the girls to be much help.

"One night at dinner, Dr. McClellan, a gifted surgeon, told us to scrub in the morning as he needed assistants in the operating room. We thought he was kidding us, but the next morning a nurse came and awakened us. 'They're ready for you in surgery,' she said. We just stood there, looking at each other.

"That was an experience. We finally scrubbed and

reported to the operating room in our gowns. My job wasn't bad, but Jim's was difficult. He had to stand across from the doctor and do whatever he was told. Since this was a hernia operation, Jim was staring into this guy's stomach the whole time. At one point, he had both hands held out, palms up, and was holding something different with each finger.

"At the next little port, we met some friends of the doctor who had a submarine chaser; it was long, narrow, and fast. They invited us to go for a little trip, and wouldn't you know, Jim accepted. There was no radio, no radar, or anything on that boat, and something was always going wrong in the engine room; it was continually catching on fire. One couldn't go up on deck as there was no railing, just a flimsy rope. Well, Jim and the children were in seventh heaven, but I had an ominous feeling.

"We went way out in the ocean, in one whale of a storm, and the boat's engine broke down. As they couldn't fix it, we were simply adrift out there. The storm was getting worse with each hour, and we were bouncing around like a cork. I never felt so helpless!

"All of us were huddled in the galley, and cans of food were flying across the room like missiles. We had no lights, as the boat's engine also drove the generator. The storm was so severe I thought we might capsize. I kept thinking, 'Dear God, how did I get in a place like this? And for what reason? For no darn good reason at all, just following Jim!'

"I was crying and praying; the kids were scared to death; Jim was trying to keep everybody calm. We spent the whole night adrift somewhere in the Pacific Ocean, praying that we wouldn't roll over. It was the longest and worst night of my life. The next day they got the engine running well enough to limp back and meet the minesweeper. That old tub never looked so good!

"On October 31, we docked at Klawock, Alaska. I

93

wanted to get off the ship and take a walk. I was fed
up with boats by then! As I got ready to go, one of the
men came up and handed me a revolver. I said,
'You've got to be kidding?' He said, 'No, Maxine, if you
go into those woods you've got to have a gun; we have
bears and wolves out there.' I said, 'That's all right, I
don't really feel like walking anyway.' "

By the time we reached Sitka, Maxine had had
enough. Jim asked her to take me back to Ketchikan
while he took my sisters farther north to view the gla-
ciers. Travel from Sitka to Ketchikan is by boat or seaplane, and Max had no desire for another boat trip.
With no other alternative, she consented to fly. Max
had no greater fear than that of flying; if given the option, she'd have preferred to make the trip by dogsled.

"That night adrift at sea," she says, "I had told God
that if he'd get me out of there alive, I'd never get on
anything dangerous again. First thing that happens,
I'm faced with flying on a rickety old seaplane with a
bush pilot.

"The morning of the flight, I was out on the dock, as
ready as I felt I could get. We waited and waited, but
they couldn't get the engine started. I inquired of
somebody, 'They can't start the engine?' He replied,
'No, and we've no idea why. It's the first time in
twenty-three years it hasn't started.' I thought, 'My
Lord, what do I do now?'

"Eventually another plane arrived; I felt better because the second plane had two engines. It was an
awful flight, rough as could be. I was sitting there,
sick as a dog, and everybody started eating lunch. The
pilot came back and jokingly offered me half his sand-
wich. I was so sick I must have looked green, but at
least we made it safely to Ketchikan."

In retrospect, incidents like this are humorous. At
the time, however, Maxine's problems were no joke,
not to the Rayburn family. Her fears weren't simply

apprehension, as one might feel before riding a roller coaster. They were more like a wave of terror-inducing anxiety. Each anxiety attack drove her deeper and deeper into her private realm of escape. On occasion Max would keep Jim up all night, pleading for more drugs.

Indeed, the problems in the Rayburn household weighed like lead, and there were few with whom we could share our pain. As Jim was a big-name Christian leader, we were in the public eye and did not dare let our problems show.

Even though I was only a young child, this confused me. If Christ loved people like us, full of failures and weaknesses, then what did we have to fear from those who profess his name? If we don't have to hide from God, then why should we have to hide from those who follow him?

A painful answer awaited me.

NINE

Frontier Ranch

ROUND UP LODGE, the prize property of the original Byrd Colonies, was a showplace used exclusively as a summer camp for wealthy boys. Located on the slopes of Mount Princeton, it was just five hundred vertical feet above Silver Cliff Ranch.

In August of 1950, eight months after the acquisition of Silver Cliff, Jim was invited to speak at Round Up Lodge for their twenty-fifth anniversary banquet. Max went with him so she could see the facility. "When the program was over," Max says, "Jim and I were in the car, winding up that little road toward the corral. Jim said, 'Max, these folks don't know it yet, but this place doesn't belong to them anymore. I asked our Father for it this evening.' "

Although Jim was unaware of it, Cy Burris and Jerry Kirk, two kids on the Silver Cliff Ranch work crew, had stumbled upon the property while on a hike and were also praying that Round Up Lodge would be given to Young Life. One month later, Dr. Marquard, the owner of Round Up, was informed by his doctor that because of a heart condition, he would need to avoid high altitude; his lodge would have to be sold. Shortly thereafter, a friend informed Jim of an ad in the *New Yorker* for a half-million-dollar boys' ranch in the Colorado Rockies. Investigation confirmed that the ad was for Round Up Lodge.

Cy, Jerry, and Jim had prayed for a miracle, and now it looked like it would come to pass. How thrilled Jim would have been if his staff had had the faith and vision of those two work-crew kids. This was not the case, however. When a couple of staff men discovered what Cy and Jerry were praying about, they told the two young men to pray more appropriately and not ask God for "stupid" things.

Jim did not tell his staff that he shared Cy's and Jerry's "foolish" idea about Round Up Lodge until he'd met with the board of directors. But the pressure of asking the board to approve this latest venture brought on yet another migraine. What if these men turned thumbs down? What would Jim do if caught between the Spirit's leading and a contradictory directive from the board? Jim described the meeting in his journal entry of January 29, 1951: *Arrived Chicago 2:45 a.m. with developing headache. In bed at LaSalle Hotel before 4:00 a.m. Up at 9:00 a.m. Pain getting worse by then. Breakfast with Gus and Millie Hill. Met Hathaways, talked to Frank Taylor, and went to Board meeting with intense migraine attack.*

A great meeting! I was bowled over in the end when

*they voted to approve the expansion project and au-
thorized me to seek the funds. By the end, I was very ill
due to headache. Somehow managed to see Coleman
Crowell and he took me to the train. Bitter cold (8° below) in Chicago. Left at 7:15 for Memphis, Tennessee.
Had to give myself a shot as train left Chicago.*

The Board meeting had fallen on Maxine's birthday.
As Jim's train left Chicago, he wrote her the following
letter.

> *Monday Evening
> En Route Memphis*

Dearest Maxie,

*This is your birthday! I feel sad because you will
think I forgot. I am writing to let you know, even
though late, that I have thought of you and remembered your birthday many times since early this morning. The Board meeting was one of the very best we
have ever had. Just before adjournment at 4:30 p.m. I
told them about Round Up Lodge. They were bowled
over! And they, in turn, bowled me over. To my utter
amazement, Mr. Taylor said that the board should au-
thorize me to contact wealthy donors and large foun-
dations for the money to buy Round Up. There was an
enthusiastic, unanimous vote authorizing me to seek
the funds. Claude, Gus, and I were naturally overjoyed!
Honey, although we haven't got Round Up by a long
shot, it was an amazing vote of confidence, and further
evidence to me of the Lord leading.*

*I had dinner with Coleman Crowell; he stayed in
town just for that. I had such pain and nausea, I just
sipped at a bowl of broth and talked to Coleman until
train time. That's the way the day went—busy, and
complicated by that terrible pain, but a wonderful day!*

*I thought of you many times. It doesn't seem possible
that you are thirty-nine. I always think of you as a little girl, like when I met you. When you're well enough*

99

to be your true self, you're still as sweet, desirable, and beautiful as you have always been. Since the first time I saw you in the Concordia Church, you have been the only girl I ever wanted. I've loved you and wanted you ever since that night. The years of illness have made it seem to you, at times, like that wasn't so, but it is.

My life was made rich by your love, especially in those blessed first years—in school—at Concordia— even at Newton and our belated honeymoon in Colorado. Best of all were the years at Chama, Douglas, Dos Cabezas, and Clifton, when you wanted so little and gave so much. I've thousands of precious memories that you gave me, of things so small you would doubt I even remember them. I couldn't have had those memories if you hadn't loved a guy starting out the hard way, at a job he didn't know how to do. I remember years when we had less materially than ever, yet we never lacked a thing, as we were so happy with each other.

Besides a million other joys, you've given me the sweetest kids in all the world. Each one of them means more to me than everything else in the world combined. So remember, darling girl, I love you! I'll bet you'll be able to pass for thirty-nine for at least another fifteen years, and ten times easier than Jack Benny can.

Yours,
Jim

Coming home was not such a warm experience as Jim's letter would imply. He and Max did well from a distance, but things were often strained when he returned. Max had lost interest in expressing herself physically. Jim would arrive and not be greeted with so much as a hug; usually, Max wouldn't even go to the door. This absence of physically expressed warmth and affection was a difficult rejection for Jim, for he truly loved Max in spite of her deep problems.

Two weeks after the Chicago board meeting, Jim informed his staff of his plans to purchase Round Up Lodge. Some wondered if he was sane. All staff salaries, including his, were low; at times, survival was a day-to-day affair. How could Jim possibly think of getting that amount of money? But Jim's faith was the product of the Spirit; he simply didn't limit God. Many Christians, he believed, fail to experience the miraculous because they never take a risk. True faith compels one to step out, to take a chance. Jim's journal for early 1951 tells of the purchase.

2/21: *A grueling but wonderful day. Arrived in Chicago at 9:00 a.m. Had meeting of trustees at Continental Bank. We went all afternoon! Talked about Round Up Lodge from every angle. It did not look too favorable when we broke up, but the Lord gave me a wonderful peace. After being violently ill, I got a good night's rest. Had to have a shot for headache—first time since the board meeting on 1/29.*

2/22: *What a day! This is the day the trustees voted to give $100,000 for the Lodge. What can I say! This is one of the greatest things the Lord ever did for me. And truly he did it all! Without him, it would be folly to attempt such things. Now to follow him for the next step.*

2/24: *The praise, thanks, peace, and joy that I am experiencing nearly overwhelm me! Never has the dear heavenly Father permitted me, in his grace, to experience so much tangible evidence of his gracious dealings and sovereign leading in my life, as in these last days. Left Colorado Springs at 5:45 a.m. Met dear friends C.H. and Hazel at Denver station. Had a precious hour with them, rejoicing together about all that is happening. Then these dear people pledged $50,000 to the Round Up Lodge Project. What can I say? They further said that if their foundation can be formed, they will*

*give $100,000 this year and next! A total of $200,000 in
two years that they hope to give! Just had time to grab
the California Zephyr at 8:40 a.m.*

*3/20: Today was the day! We closed the deal for Round
Up Lodge after a long, hard day with Dr. Marquard.
What can I possibly say? The Lord God is so wonderful
and has done such a super, abundant thing for us. I
want always to praise and thank him! Talked to Crowell trustees, also to Mr. Wetmore, Mr. Weyerhauser,
Mr. Mitchell, and Mr. Gillis. All agreed we go ahead! A
great spirit of oneness!*

*Mrs. Paulsen made a splendid pledge today to take
us over $300,000.*

Less than seven months had passed since Jim told
Maxine that Round Up Lodge would soon be in his
hands, because he had asked the Father for it that
evening. At that time, it wasn't for sale. There wasn't
even any plan to sell it.

Those who had watched the miraculous acquisition
of these beautiful resorts were amazed. It seemed as if
Jim's next trick would be to walk on water. Everything the man envisioned, no matter how absurd it
seemed, came to pass. Star Ranch, Silver Cliff Ranch,
and Round Up Lodge—now Frontier Ranch—had all
been acquired in the short span of four years. They
were all showplaces; indeed, they were the fanciest
camps in the country. People who had scoffed at Jim
found themselves with "egg on the face." Wally Howard says, "We questioned his wanting to get the camp
properties, but every time, we enjoyed them as much
as he did. Sometimes we felt embarrassed that we
were receiving all these benefits that none of us were
qualified to visualize or to go out and get. I decided
that I would never again question Jim's telling us the
Lord was laying it on his heart to get more property."

Frontier Ranch was indeed special to Jim. It was his idea of God's sanctuary, an awe-inspiring, mighty expanse of majestic beauty. Located on the backbone of the great continental divide and nestled in the splendor of cathedral-like cliffs towering one thousand feet above her, Frontier Ranch became Jim's lover. She restored him, rebuilt him, and sent him off to battle with a soft kiss. His residence there was known as the Lookout. It was the only place he ever called home. Those summers spent in the Lookout were the happiest times of his life. The awesome beauty of the place seemed an appropriate match to Jim's awesome faith and lifestyle. It was wonderful to see my father so fulfilled. Life had thrown a lot of problems in his direction, and the Lookout seemed to be God's way of providing him a special refuge.

A former staff man recalls: "Jim should have lived there year around. There was such a warm, special aura to the place when he was in residence. That aura hasn't been evident since he left. It's almost like the Lookout misses Jim as much as he missed it. He was so meticulous about the place; there were flowers everywhere, beautiful manicured lawns, and people coming and going. The place seemed to be alive. Today, those flower beds are full of weeds, and the lawns are gone—just patches of dirt. Something is missing, or should I say, somebody is missing."

103

At Frontier Ranch, Jim introduced thousands of kids to one of his favorite sports, snow sliding. High in the majestic Rockies, at an elevation of about 13,000 feet, he would find a snow cornice, a place where the prevailing winter winds blowing across a high ridge created an overhang, or ledge, of snow. The ideal cornice would have a twenty- to thirty-foot vertical drop onto a steeply inclined snow field.

After finding the best location, Jim would gather the crowd, give a minimal set of instructions, and slowly start inching out on the cornice while everybody watched. When the snow could no longer support his weight, he simply disappeared through a small hole, screaming and hollering all the way. It was a weird experience if you were following him and didn't really understand what was happening, since there was no way for those left standing on the ridge to see below. Jim's fate remained a question mark. One had only the memory of his scream fading away as he dropped a thousand feet into the valley below, and the small hole through which he'd disappeared.

The most difficult position was to be the next in line. Not knowing for sure if Jim was dead or alive, person number two would reluctantly inch toward the edge of the cornice. Eventually, when he was about to change his mind, the snow would give way—*whoosh!* Another scream, another small hole, and the third person in line now stood there alone, an apprehensive look on his face.

It was all a matter of physics, as Jim explained to many a skeptic. There was little shock to one's body after the fall, as the snow field below the cornice was extremely steep. After landing on the snow, one could slide a thousand feet down the mountain in thirty seconds. The real danger was the emotional trauma felt by those who didn't share Jim's zest for adventure.

Snow sliding was a thrilling sport. The kids who tried it became instant enthusiasts, making as many trips down the mountain as they had strength for. Overcoming beginner's fear served to make the whole experience more exciting. A former snow slider says:

"We used to return from the snow slides with Jim driving in front, and all the trucks and buses, loaded with kids, strung out behind. At one point, he'd pull over to the side of the road and the whole caravan would come to a halt, waiting for Jim to reveal a problem. Then, just like a madman, he'd go running across to the river, trip and fall, and come up dripping and spluttering, waving for everyone to join him. It must have confused many a tourist, or fisherman, when three hundred kids emptied from the buses and ran pell-mell into the ice cold river. I'd be so cold from snow sliding that that stream actually warmed me up."

Another of Jim's loves was exploring old mines. He had graduate credits in geology and was well aware of which mines were safe and which were not. There was nothing he loved more than taking a group of kids deep into the belly of the earth to show them the ins and outs of gold and silver mining. He also loved mountain climbing. Dr. "Chubby" Andrews remembers:

"Jim was one of those fellas peculiarly built for mountain climbing, with his sort of bow legs, and his feet that seemed to grab hold of the side of a mountain. He looked like a billy goat climbing right on up to the peak. There wasn't anything he was afraid to tackle.

"That rascal Rayburn said, 'Chub, I know a lake up there on top of the mountain that's just loaded with trout. You bring your rod and we'll catch 'em.' But he just wanted me to hike up that mountain with him! It was a beautiful place, but I didn't catch a fish. He had a way of making it fun, regardless. His enthusiasm just swept you into whatever he had in mind. . . . It captivated you."

When mountain climbing, snow sliding, jeeping, camping, or exploring mines, no one could match Jim's rapport with kids. Nor could anyone present Jesus Christ to young adults as effectively as he could. But for all his gifts, Jim could be stubbornly rigid, unbending in his viewpoints. Such was the case in the controversy over program at Frontier Ranch.

At the Presbyterian camps in Arizona, Jim had been

trained to schedule lots of meetings and a mandatory nap time after lunch. Although he wouldn't pay a dime to know what Presbyterians thought about running a camp for kids, on this one issue he clung to their viewpoint as if it were written in stone. Bob Mitchell recalls:

"The wake-up bell would ring, and the campers would have twenty minutes to get down to a thing called 'The Huddle.' This was before breakfast; they weren't even awake yet. We'd give two work-crew kids the responsibility of leading a song and giving a testimony. That was the most difficult assignment any human being ever had. Those kids would sit there, half asleep, starting their day with a religious meeting. The only reason we got away with it was that those work-crew kids were so attractive.

"Then the campers would go to breakfast, and right back to their cabins again. 'Do not pass Go, do not collect $200.' Don't have any fun. Right back to your cabin to clean that dude up, because inspection came next. If your cabin got below three points, you did the dishes, and Jim would personally reprimand the counselor. After the cleanup, we'd herd them right smack dab into a meeting called the Morning Roundup, which was singing and speaking.

"That was the job for the second best speaker in camp. Jim would take the night assignment, and he would give the up-and-coming men, the learners, the morning spot.

"By eleven o'clock in the morning we'd had two meetings, a cleanup, and a meal inside, and there's the beautiful Colorado sunshine outside, and the kids have hardly been out yet. So we'd stick in a little bit of free time before lunch, and open the pool.

"After lunch, from the moment you walked out the dining-hall door, it was Silence! You couldn't say a word. Just go back to your cabin and lie down for one

Right: A 1930 photo of Maxine Stanley, beauty queen of Kansas State University.

Below: The Community Presbyterian Church of Chama, New Mexico, in 1934, where Jim and Maxine launched their career.

Above: Rayburn family portrait at Star Ranch, taken in 1948.
From left to right: Jim, Jim III, Ann, "Captain" the dog,
Maxine, Sue.

Right: Jim and Maxine at the Lookout, Frontier Ranch, 1952.
Photo by Rudy Vetter.

Jim at
high
school
hangout
in 1949.

Kids
from
Jim's
North
Dallas
High
School
Club,
1943.

Volunteers rush to fight the forest fire that had encircled
Star Ranch in 1950.

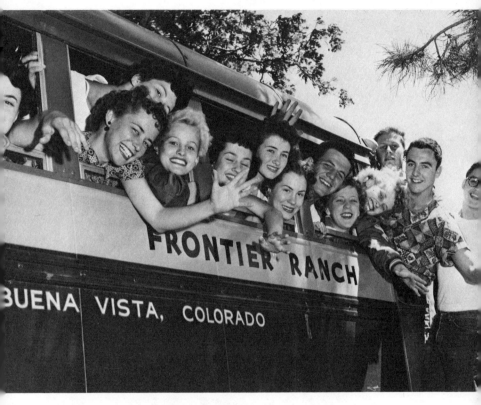

Campers leaving Frontier Ranch for the snow slides, high on the Continental Divide in Colorado (1953).

Left: On the cable over Chalk Creek, en route to the snow slides.

Right: Jim's people loved a laugh. Here, George Sheffer does his scarecrow routine.

Below: Andrew "Goldbrick" Delaney, whose only policy manual was a loving heart, serves up barbecue in a Colorado aspen grove.

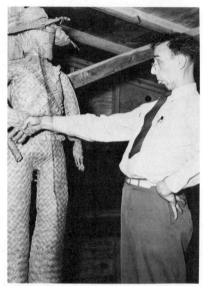

Upper left: Sue Rayburn, age 14, outside the Lookout at Frontier Ranch. Photo by Rudy Vetter.

Upper right: From left to right: Bob Mitchell, Dick Lowey, and Phil McDonald pursue Jim down the gravel slide at Frontier Ranch.

Above: Kids at Frontier Ranch enjoy a wrangler's breakfast in the Colorado Rockies.

Overleaf: Nearly five hundred kids filled the mortuary parlor for Jim's Tuesday night meetings (1956).

Insets: Jim, amid mountains that matched his vision, skiing the Swiss Alps in 1954, and practicing the slalom at the Castaway Club, Detroit Lakes, Minnesota.

Left: Jim, hamming it up for the kids and demonstrating the finer points of mountain climbing safety, atop the Kissing Camels, Garden of the Gods, Colorado Springs, Colorado.

Above: Jim at the Malibu Club in British Columbia, Canada, 1959.

Right: Excited and awe-struck guests being welcomed at the Malibu Club, Jim's incredible resort for kids in the Canadian wilderness.

Contemplating the horror and seeking his Father's leading, Jim strolls alongside the Berlin Wall in 1963.

solid hour. And there was the Colorado sunshine out there, and we still hadn't gotten out in it. Finally, in the afternoon, we'd have about three hours of activities. Then dinner, and right after dinner would be the counselors' meeting. Then we'd herd the kids into the Roundup, and those were great nights. The kids loved those night meetings! They were fun; they saved the day!

"But after the night meeting, more times than not, we'd have a second meeting. That would be a Moody science film with a Christian message, or a work-crew testimonial night, or some other after-meeting type of message. After everything was over, there was the seventh meeting. Back to your cabin for 'Cabin Time,' like group discussions."

For those kids with red blood in their systems, seven meetings and a nap was too much to take. Many protested to their counselors, and in turn, the counselors came to Jim.

"Those kids are wrong," Jim would argue. "They don't know what is right. Are you leaders, or aren't you?"

So much of Christ's message deals with relationships, and few could present that message like Jim, yet his own inability to relate closely with his staff, to be more flexible, was slowly driving a wedge between Jim and his people. Most of his followers, at one time or another, felt Jim didn't care about them, that they were expendable. Much pain, on both sides of the fence, was caused by poor communication.

The emphasis received in childhood to be good, to make people proud, to live a life beyond reproach had made it difficult for Jim to deal with criticism. Censure was a very personal thing for him; to be criticized was to be disliked, and that hurt him deeply. At times Jim's true feelings bubbled to the surface, sin or no sin. Norm Robbins says, "I remember an early staff

107

conference at Star Ranch where Jim broke down and wept, right in front of the whole group. The reason? He'd heard talk about his being difficult to get close to. It just wiped him out! I'm sure he was most misunderstood."

Underneath Jim's stern exterior lived the heart of a puppy. Outwardly he gave the impression of self-sufficiency, almost cockiness. In his heart, however, he was deeply aware of his shortcomings.

At the ranches during the summer, many of Jim's followers were awed and strengthened by Jim's commitment to prayer. When discouragement plagued them, Jim would get a few men together and say, "We're gonna get the horses and ride up Mt. Princeton to the saddle." He would take four or five men at a time, and they would pray all night. Says Bob Reeverts: "First time I went I couldn't believe it! I'd camped out before, but pray all night? I didn't know what to think! It was easy to stay awake; it was cold! We'd rustle up some hot coffee and just pray. Words fail to express what those times came to mean."

On other occasions, Jim called his people together for three days, sometimes a week, of prayer. A staff member recalls: "At the time I thought, 'How in the world can I spend three days praying? This is crazy!' But we did, and Jim kept us right at it. He didn't mess around. He'd say, 'Well, boys, we're here to pray. We're here to pray.' Those turned out to be some very special times."

While in summer residence at the Lookout, Jim's creative hosting of adult guests launched his work into a new era. From governors and senators to the popcorn vendor at the local rodeo, the great and the small came to taste his hospitality. Exposing guests to the kids, the facilities, and the program was Jim's avocation. A gracious host, he was well known for loading visitors into his convertible or jeep and disappearing for a day in his beloved mountains.

This constant exposure to new people in every walk of life moved Jim into a higher realm of thinking and planning. In a sense, he was outgrowing his own people.

TEN
Gold

WHILE Jim was on a trip to Philadelphia, May 4, 1951, at the Harvey Cedars Conference Grounds, God led him to a huge pocket òf "gold." No prospector ever made a richer strike. This find was destined to bless Jim's work for a quarter century.

Andrew "Goldbrick" Delaney and his wife, Jerry, were cooking for a kids' camp run by Norm Robbins. As employees of Parker Woolmington, who owned the catering service Norm had hired for the weekend, they knew nothing about Jim, Norm, or Young Life. Jerry recalls:

"We were busy in the kitchen when Jim walked in,

grabbed a piece of chicken, and walked out. I asked
Andy if he knew who the guy was, and he said he
didn't. No doubt it was someone who thought himself
a V.I.P. Before long, here he comes again, but this
time he looked all sheepish and reluctant. Jim stood
there for a minute with those St. Bernard eyes, and finally asked us if he could have some more chicken.

"Next thing you know, he's asking us if we'd come
to work for him in a big kids' camp back in Colorado.
We said no, so he said he was going to put us on his
prayer list. Andy and I looked at each other, both
knowing what the other was thinking. 'This guy's
crazy. Put us on a prayer list? What's a prayer list?'

"Well, we didn't know what it was like to be in Jim's
prayers. Several days later Parker, our boss, went to
Colorado to work for Jim, and we were out of a job.
So Andy wrote Jim a letter, and the very next month
we pulled into Colorado to join his staff. We fed 'em,
and Jim talked to 'em; together, we were quite a
team."

It was not an easy transition for Goldbrick and Jerry
to leave their families and go west to Colorado. Theirs
were the only black faces on a very white Young Life
landscape. The first few years were lonely, as few
doors opened to welcome them. But for the Rayburn
family, Goldbrick and Jerry arrived like two angels in
the night. With Jim on the road much of the time, and
Maxine frequently out of commission, Goldbrick and
Jerry finished raising the three Rayburn kids. Without
their help in so many areas, I'm not sure we'd have
made it through the long, dark tunnel.

I never heard my black foster parents talk of Christ.
However, I saw them live Christ, day in and day out,
for twenty-five years. They saw the Rayburn family as
we really were, warts and all, and never lost their love
or respect for us. I never heard them complain or gos-

112

sip, although they, more than anyone else, had ample justification to do both.

One of the highlights of Jim's weeks at Frontier came on each camp's opening night. That's when he introduced the kids to "the greatest kids' chef in the world," Andrew "Goldbrick" Delaney. Brick would stroll into the dining room with his tall white chef's hat and wave his big black hand, and four hundred kids would go crazy. There was no higher honor for work-crew kids at Frontier Ranch than being assigned to the kitchen or dining room. They were the chosen few who worked with the Delaneys. Kids from every corner of this globe and almost every state in the U.S. have spent a week singing "Hurrah for Goldbrick."

Goldbrick and Jerry caught Jim's vision and lived by it. Jim referred to Brick as his vice-president. He and Jerry embody the true spirit of friendship evangelism, and they'll be doing kids' work till their homecoming. Both left Young Life in the late seventies to open Delaney's Depot, a restaurant in Buena Vista, Colorado.

Speaking for the Rayburn family and countless thousands of others, I can say that our life was richer and much blessed by having Goldbrick and Jerry to show us the higher road. They were as much Young Life as Jim, and they will never be forgotten.

113

E L E V E N

Malibu Resort

WHEN the Young Life staff first got wind that
Jim was off in the wilds of Canada looking at a fourth
campsite, their ability to think big was stretched to the
breaking point. Even though some had vowed never
to question him again, adding a resort in the Canadian wilderness was pushing things too far.

The whole adventure got started in the spring of
1952. Add Sewell, one of the Young Life pioneers from
Dallas Seminary, and his wife, Loveta, invited their lo-
cal automobile dealer, Jim Campbell, to join them and
Jim for the evening. Campbell got to talking about the
Malibu Club, a fabulous million-dollar resort where

he had been a guest, somewhere up the inland waterway beyond Vancouver. He mentioned that it was for sale.

Tucked among remote fjords in British Columbia, the resort was fully furnished, even after sitting vacant for a year. Draperies and bedspreads of finest quality were still in the rooms. According to Campbell, even the dining room was still set for guests who seem to have hastily departed.

Campbell had been dreaming for some time of turning this escape for Hollywood greats into an elegant high-school resort for Young Life. He pulled out some photos of the Malibu Club and talked Jim and Add into flying up the inlet the next day to check out the mystery property. From Jim's journal: *This was a pleasant, restful, thrilling day. Flew in Campbell's Seabee to Malibu Club in Canada. Spectacular place.*

Malibu was elegantly perched on primordial rock jutting into the cold deep waters of the Princess Louisa inlet. It was a hundred miles north of Vancouver, beyond the reach of ordinary transportation, lost in the pine forested mountains, and known chiefly to lumbermen and wealthy West Coast yachters. When the Young Life board first discovered that Jim was looking at some property that one couldn't get to except by water, they told him, "Jim, boats are just not safe." And in his characteristic manner he drawled, "Well, I'm sure glad the Alaska Steamship Company never heard of that!"

A year and a half after his first visit to Malibu, Jim met Tom Hamilton, the owner, to talk about a possible purchase. These were still days when staff folks were lucky to find a nickel in their jeans. To consider purchasing a piece of property worth a million dollars seemed preposterous. But mixed in with fear that a new resort might be sheer presumption was confidence in past history which proved God's phenomenal

leading through Jim's vision and leadership. Late in
1953 Jim wrote:

11/2: *Felt "low" and generally bad ... worried about
tonight and ashamed that I am.*

11/3: *A wonderful conference with Hamilton. Am right
in feeling like Malibu is about to be ours. I humbly
thank God for all he is doing.*

11/4: *Looks better all the time. I seem to have a sense
of the Lord's sovereignty and omniscience in this. How
little I have done. Nothing! But wonderful things continue to happen, things I believe God initiates.*

11/5: *Tom Hamilton came while I was breakfasting. ...
We quickly got into the Malibu deal and signed the
agreement binding him to sell at the phenomenal price
of $300,000, and binding me only to* try. *He is willing
to take $150,000 down. How I do thank God. I've sel-
dom felt so deeply grateful to him.*

Three days later, Jim, Add Sewell, Jim Campbell,
and Bill Starr flew into Malibu for one final look at the
property. Bill recalls, "The thought that overwhelmed
my mind as we toured the place was that Jim spoke
as if Malibu was ours, as though it was an accomplished fact ... and I thought we were just flying up to
look at it."

117

Since Hamilton had asked for the deal to be con-
summated by the end of 1953, to allow him an income
tax advantage, Jim saw that he had seven weeks to try
for the money. He wasted no time. A whirlwind travel
schedule covering 23,000 miles, twenty-five cities, and
hundreds of contacts, mixed with many miracles, led
to this December 21 entry in his journal: *A most his-
toric day! We went into escrow on the Malibu transac-
tion this morning! Everybody very happy! The Lord*

has been wonderfully good in permitting us great forward strides.

To some it seemed that Jim had pulled another rabbit from his hat. Could he really walk on water, or maybe feed a whole camp on just one hamburger? For some of Jim's staff, admiration for the boss gave way to adoration, and a dangerous die was cast. When one human being deifies another, there is trouble ahead.

Jim was not deceived about the source of his power. Here are his thoughts on hero worship:

The best I know, I go where God leads, but oftentimes I do not know. I have to rely on the fact that he is great enough and good enough to guide me. And when he does guide me, he is also great enough to get me where he wants me. I am a feeble being. I don't know God's plans. It is sad to me when someone tries to figure out God's plan. I can think and earnestly pray, but in the final analysis I have to go back to this glorious, revealed fact: God is here! He is here to see me through and committed to seeing that I stay in his path. Paul said that God is able to make his grace abound towards us, that we will always have a sufficiency.

God is able; I am unable. I'm a weakling. I'm blind. I can't figure out his way nor can I see ahead. But recognizing that we are not able to find God's way is probably the first reaction our hearts need in connection with the leadership of God's spirit. He takes special care of weaklings! "My grace is sufficient for thee: for my strength is made perfect in weakness" [2 Cor. 12:9, KJV]. He rejoices to move us along in his divine pattern when we come to him, weak, hopeless, and helpless in ourselves. Go day by day, through every trying decision, with this great sovereignty of God in the forefront of your mind. I am God's. God will lead. He has given his Word. He will not let go of me.

I am utterly disgusted with this tendency to worship human leaders. I wanted to swat a guy recently over some things he said concerning me. He missed the whole point by trying to pour a little anointing oil on Jim Rayburn. He gave the picture the wrong slant. If I have anything at all, I received it from God. If I differ in any way from others, it's only because God has touched me. We have no right to be bowing to anybody and saying, "Oh, isn't he wonderful." Who's wonderful? Jesus Christ is!

My friend, if it so happens that one of God's servants has taken the gifts given him and has so lived out Christ that the glory of the Lord Jesus shows through the dull clay of that human vessel, then do you know who you ought to praise? Jesus Christ! Not that clay vessel. The vessel's just in the way. Jesus Christ just shows a little bit through the human clay of our lives. He doesn't really show in the fullness of his splendor. What a silly idea, bowing down and worshiping an old vessel of clay. That old cracked pot won't do any good. All right, then, let's not worship cracked pots. That'll make us all crackpots.

TWELVE

Preacher man

BY 1952, Jim's Young Life club in Colorado Springs was drawing from three to four hundred kids per week. And this in an era when most churches were fortunate to have a dozen kids in their high-school program! Finding a meeting place adequate for four hundred people was no small problem, as Jim refused to hold his meetings in a church. The solution? Funeral homes.

Loud music poured from the parlor room at the local mortuary every Tuesday night at 7:30. One of the favorite songs contained the line, "He lives, he lives, . . . he walks with me, he talks with me. . . ." Legend has it that passing pedestrians were more than a little startled by such music emanating from a mortuary.

What magic brought out such numbers of typically uninterested kids to hear about Jesus Christ? What did Jim tell them; why would they listen? A typical message follows:

Almost everybody's heard about Jesus Christ. It would be hard to imagine that any rational person in the United States of America didn't know the name of Jesus Christ. The reason? It's probably the most common curse word in all the world! One of the names of the Savior is used more often than any other name for cursing. Isn't that a terrible thing? Most people never stop and think how incongruous that is. Jesus never hurt anybody; he never did anything wrong. You can scrutinize his life as carefully as you want to, but you cannot find anything that isn't admirable.

Jesus was the kind of a man we men would like to be and can't be, 'cause we haven't got the guts. He was the kind of man you girls would like your man to be, but he'll never be that. He won't be as courageous, he won't be as gentle, he won't be as compassionate, he won't be as loving, he won't be as tender, he won't be as manly as Jesus Christ. And yet if you hit your finger with a hammer or want somebody to think you're real tough, you usually blurt out the name of Jesus, or Christ. In some connection, in some dirty way, you use the dearest name that ever was.

That's what your gang does at your school, isn't it? And I'm not picking on just your school. Saturday night I'll be talking to kids in Philadelphia; I won't even know what school they go to, but I can say it just as easily, because it happens in every school. If you want to peddle some dirty gossip, or tell a dirty lie, or defame somebody's character, or do something that's

122

*ugly, you almost always use the name of Jesus Christ
in connection with it.*

*Did you ever think of that? Right down at your
school! Come and tell me if it isn't so; you'll break a
record. I've told several hundred thousand kids, "That's
what they do at your school, isn't it?" Nobody ever
comes and tells me, "Jim, you're wrong, they don't do
that at our school. Nobody ever says bad things about
girls at our school. Nobody uses the name of Jesus or
Christ. Why, we wouldn't think of doing that!" Not
one! You see, I'm so right I don't have to worry about
anybody saying that. I'd be shocked clean outa my
shoes if somebody came and said I was wrong, 'cause
I've been right for so long. But it's terrible to be so
right, so right about such a terrible thing.*

*Tomorrow when you hear somebody blurt out a
bunch of filthy conversation, and it has the name of the
Savior mixed up in it, you probably won't think much
about it. We're used to ugly things. We've got dirty insides. That's why I'd hate to have to be good enough
for God. I've got dirty insides. We've all got dirty insides!*

*We don't put God in the right place. We don't respect
human life and human personality, or we wouldn't
lightly mix up the dearest and sweetest things with the
ugliest things. No real person would, man or woman.
We don't get things in their right place. The only people, I believe, that ever get 'em in the right place—get
right and wrong, good and bad, things that count and
things that don't count, things that build up and things
that tear down—the only people that ever get things in
the right place are the people who have Jesus Christ in
the right place.*

*There's a mysterious thing that happens when you
get properly related to Jesus Christ through this trust-
ing business, believing on him the way the Bible says.*

123

Then something happens inside of you, something God does. You don't have to struggle with it. It comes from God. It makes new life because it actually is a new life. It makes new life possible for you because it's a new life in you.

I want to take three witnesses tonight, three of my great heroes, three of the greatest men who ever lived— Peter, John, and Paul. They weren't great at all until they met Jesus Christ! He made 'em great! They're perfect illustrations of how Jesus Christ can take common, ordinary people, like you and me, and make 'em great. Take Peter, for instance. He was a "blunderbuss" sort of a fellow—probably a loudmouth, a fellow who spoke first and thought later. What he said was usually wrong. He was a fisherman. Doesn't take too many brains to be a fisherman. Even I can catch fish. There wasn't anything famous about him; he was just a common, ordinary, workin' boy, that's all. One day Jesus came by, stopped Peter, and had Peter come with him. I'll leave it with you, when you get interested in history, to find somebody that made a greater mark than Peter. I know two or three, but Peter stands up at the head of the human race as one of the greatest men ever produced. You'd have never heard of him if it hadn't been for Jesus Christ! Never woulda heard of him!

124

Now John was a friend of Peter; he was in the same business. From the nickname Jesus gave him, Son of Thunder, I wouldn't be surprised but what John was a loudmouth too. That may have been a loudmouth mob down there on the Sea of Galilee. You can't tell, but I kinda believe they were. But they were always on the sea; there weren't too many people around, so they could make all the noise they wanted.

Now, John. You don't know beans about John, his background and all. Nobody else does either. John was the son of Zebedee. Yeah, but who ever heard of Zebedee? We wouldn't even know that John was the son of

Zebedee if it wasn't for John; Zebedee never did anything! All in the world he gets credit for is being John's
old man. Just think that over for a minute—you may
come up with something. John wouldn't be anybody
but the son of Zebedee, and Zebedee wasn't anybody
that people ever heard of, if it hadn't been for Jesus
Christ. Who is John now? Because he met Jesus Christ,
he's one of the greatest loved, one of the most impres-
sive, and one of the most majestic figures in the whole
human race. You can go to great cathedrals and find
them named after John—the Cathedral of St. John the
Divine. Now he'd just faint if he'd heard 'em callin' him
Saint John the Divine, 'cause he was just a common,
ordinary boy like you and me. Only thing is, he met Jesus Christ, and Jesus Christ made a wonderful person
outa him. He'll do that for you, too. But John was no
more a saint than I am. Nobody calls me Saint Jim.

   Now Paul wasn't a nobody; Paul was a somebody,
that is, in a certain circle. These two boys, Peter and
John, they were just nobodies; they were just kinda
bums down there on the Sea of Galilee, catchin' fish
and horsin' around—talking a lot. But Paul, he was a
leading citizen of Damascus. Now I'll ask you just one
question. Outside of Paul, just name me one other leading citizen of Damascus. [Pause] You can't do it! Paul
was a prominent fellow; he was a leading man in the
synagogue. He was a very religious sort of person. But
we'd have never heard of Paul if it hadn't been for Jesus Christ. All the other leading citizens of Damascus
have long since gone down the drain. We can hardly
remember where Damascus was, and we wouldn't
know about Damascus at all if it wasn't for Paul. Paul
put Damascus on the map. But he wasn't great, great
enough to stand at the head of the human race, until
Jesus Christ came into his heart.

   Jesus Christ, the Savior. He makes life work. Now a
lot of you say, "Oh yes, I believe in him all right," and

125

then you go on acting like you didn't. John says that if you say you love God, and hate somebody, you're a liar. You see? He wipes out this idea that you can be a Christian simply by saying, "Oh yes, I've done this and I've done that; oh yes, I belong to the church; oh yes, I believe in Jesus Christ." A person who has really put his trust in Jesus Christ has a new life. It came to him from God; he's not a Christian because of anything he did.

Peter, John, and Paul—if you trace the secret of their success, you'll find the reason they were great was that they saw what Jesus Christ had done for them. You can't pick up a Bible without seeing that. For—that's just a common little old preposition, but it's also one of the biggest words in the language. I don't care if you belong to every church in town, if you're the nicest boy or girl in your high school; I don't care if your name is above reproach, if you don't know the meaning of for, if you don't know what Jesus Christ has done for you, then you're not a Christian, and you're kiddin' yourself if you think you are! You don't know what life is all about, and you haven't even started to live yet. You're messin' around with some kind of counterfeit article, 'cause life begins with Christ. What do you believe Jesus did for you? All the people I know that have been changed, like Peter, John, and Paul, believe one thing— I don't care whether they're Catholic, Jewish, or Protestant; I don't care what color their skin is; I don't care how much education they've had—they all believe that Jesus Christ did somethin' for us that we could never have done for ourselves.

Jesus did somethin' tremendous for me, so much that when I think of it the teardrops start; so much that I'll never be able to thank him; so much that it wouldn't make any difference if I never had another happy moment, if I could just please him, and honor him, and show him how thankful I am. He suffered for me, the just for the unjust, to free me from the curse of death and give me a new life.

I'll close with a tragic and fascinating illustration from the Gospels. You know the day they took Jesus Christ into Pilate's Hall, into that crazy kangaroo court with all those trumped-up charges which nobody believed, and actually got a death sentence pronounced on the only man in the world that never deserved any punishment. When all this happened, there was at the same time a man in death row waiting for his execution. He had one chance to be set free. There was a strange Jewish custom that the Romans observed, that anybody who was sentenced to death, prior to the feast of the Passover, was eligible to be set free. The Jewish religious leaders could pick out any person guilty of a crime that had the death penalty, and they'd set him free, as a part of the celebration of the feast.

The man in jail was named Barabbas. Barabbas was a murderer; he had been in an insurrection, and he was guilty of murder during this insurrection. He was in death row, and he was about to be executed. The chief priests and the elders persuaded the crowd that they should ask freedom for Barabbas and destroy Jesus. The governor said, "Which of the two will you that I release unto you?" And they all said, "Barabbas." Pilate said to them, "What then shall I do with Jesus?" And they yelled, "Crucify him." You and I are members of the same human race that did that; they had a choice between a murderer and Jesus Christ, the Savior. We have the choice, we human beings. Whom will you have? Barabbas or Jesus?

127

Now don't you ever stop and think, "I wouldn't have done anything like that." Do you know who those people were? Those were some of the finest people in Jerusalem. Those were the respected, trusted, religious leaders of the city. Anybody who puts himself in the place where Christ is supposed to be, anybody who

says that he is good enough for God and doesn't ac-
knowledge that he needs Jesus Christ, is guilty of yelling "crucify him," or yelling for a murderer to be
saved, instead of Jesus. All right! The murderer was set
free. Just look at ole Barabbas, cringing in death row,
shiverin' and shakin' and wonderin' when they are
gonna knock on his door. And just think of him as the
clamor comes down the hall, and the door is jerked
open, and the soldiers kick him out. "Get outa here—
you're set free—they chose you to be set free. They had
somebody who was really somebody to free, and they
chose you instead. You dirty bum."

They took Jesus, led him up to a place outside the city
called Golgotha, the place of the skull. Dirty, ugly
name. They took him up there, pounded spikes in his
hands and feet, and hung him on a cross to die. God
says, "for you, for me." Paul says, "He died for me."
Peter says, "He suffered for me." John says, "God gave
him for us." There was one fellow in town that day
who really understood what that meant.

Barabbas was free; he coulda been there. If he was
there, I can almost see him, lookin' up at that cross,
lookin' at that one he didn't know. Jesus had been
beaten, he'd been spit on, he'd had a crown of thorns
pressed down on his head, he was blood smeared, he
was such a beat-up mess he didn't even look like a human. But there he hung, up there on the cross, sus-
pended between heaven and earth, for you and for me.
All the weight of his dear body hanging on those ugly
spike wounds, and this Barabbas, walkin' around the
cross. What do you suppose he was thinking?

Barabbas was the one man in Jerusalem who knew
what it meant for someone to die in his place. I like to
stand in his shoes and look up at the Savior. Jesus was
bloody, beaten by men of my own race, religious men,
well-reared men, like I was, men who thought they
were good enough for God and could get along with-

128

out a Savior. And I say to you kids, I don't see how you
can leave him out. I don't see how you can act like you
don't love him and don't care about him. I should
think he'd make so much difference to you, you
couldn't stand it, and you'd rush to thank him for
what he's done. But you can't walk out of here saying,
"Jim's right, I'm going to be a better person," 'cause
that's not what I'm saying.

   This would be a good time for you to pray, a real
good time. "Well, Lord, I just never have done anything
about this, I never have settled it. Jesus died for me all
that long time ago, and he's given me sixteen or seven-
teen years of good life on this earth, and I've never
given him one thing. I've never even thanked him for
dying for me."

   "But as many as received him, to them gave he
power to become the sons of God, even to them that believe on his name." See? If you believe this, really believe it 'way down deep in your heart, he'll bring you
new life, he'll make you right with God. He'll give you
a wonderful, wonderful treasure. Jesus said, "Behold, I
stand at the door, and knock: if any man hear my
voice, and open the door, I will come in." You got
ahold of the handle; you wanna open the door? Jesus
Christ will come in as soon as you open the door. He's
there. He's there knockin'. He's there waitin'.

THIRTEEN

Compassion

CHRISTIANITY began in a great adventure. In those first days when the Master was presenting his way of living to men who had vision and courage enough to try it, discipleship was a costly spiritual exploit. The life to which Jesus summoned men required insight and bravery to undertake and fortitude to continue. Who at first could have dreamed that it ever would become in the eyes of multitudes a stiff and finished system to be passively received?

Faith in the New Testament was a matter of personal venturesomeness. It involved self-committal, devotion, loyalty, and courage. It was not faith in formal creeds, for no creeds had yet been written; it was not faith in the New Testament, for the New Testament was not yet in existence; it was not faith in the church, for the church was as yet inchoate and unorganized. It was a vital and dynamic personal relationship with Christ through his indwelling Spirit.

In the faith of the early church, the Spirit was the central reality. Faith was not a conviction for thought or a matter of instructed dogma. It sprang directly from vivid, commanding, indubitable experience. Today, so many are enslaved in a Spiritless counterfeit "Christianity," that people led of God's Spirit are frequently viewed as rebels, dreamers, or heretics. Jim was burdened for those who didn't know this spiritual experience. It weighed on his heart that children grow into adulthood without understanding who Jesus is or what he has done for them. He later realized that some on his staff had never had a spiritual encounter. In a mid-fifties speech to his co-workers, he said, "I've enough people in this room to turn the world upside down for Jesus Christ, *if* they were born-of-Spirit Christians."

Jim's experience of the Holy Spirit produced in him a compassion for young people that he earnestly wished to communicate to his staff. In this talk, he speaks about his experience and Jesus' compassionate example.

132

Much to my surprise, I've found in going around the country that so many people on the staff of Young Life never had any kind of experience like I did, and for that matter didn't know about mine. And so it's been awhile now that I've thought we should talk more about theology—the glorious truths concerning our faith. So far as I am concerned, personally, there would have been no Young Life work at all without Dr. Lewis Chafer's course in soteriology.

My whole life was completely changed when I found out the Holy Spirit was a real person—God, living in my life, doing things for me that I could never do myself. I read in God's word that men's eyes are to be filled with the person and the glory of the Lord Jesus Christ, and it is the Holy Spirit's business to make it so—only he can make it so. Bow down to the influences of the Spirit, bow down and open your heart to all his wonderful person and leadership, and your gaze will be concentrated on Jesus Christ.

The greatest thing about the Lord Jesus Christ while he was on his way to the cross to die for our sins was his treatment of people—all kinds of folks. I am particularly interested in the phrase, "Jesus was moved with compassion." He saw a crowd of people and he was moved with compassion. He felt sorry for those people. His heart went out to them. Compassion is warmth, an entering in, a heartfelt desire to be on their side. Jesus saw the multitude, and they looked like scattered sheep. A pitiful sight—blundering, stumbling sheep. He had pity, he had love, he had warmth, but compassion is even more than that. He had sympathy—sympathy for their plight, and sympathy for their viewpoint.

The Lord Jesus was never cross, he was never surprised by people's evil ways. Only two things ever surprised Jesus. A young fellow from a pagan country really trusted him. He had a servant desperately ill, and he came to Jesus and mentioned this fact. Jesus decided to go to his house, remember? The young officer of the Roman army said, "No, don't come down to my house," and he gave two of the most amazing reasons you ever heard. He said first of all, "I'm not even worthy that you should come under my roof," and second, "You don't need to. You can take care of the healing by remote control. You're in charge of life; you run the whole business." I don't know how that Roman officer knew that. I'm sure he didn't find it out in Rome. He

133

was an officer of the occupying army, yet he knew it. And Jesus was astonished! He hadn't seen faith like that anywhere, even among his own people. On another occasion he was astonished that the people didn't believe. After all the works he did, after all the evidence was in, they still didn't believe. Remember that! Unbelief and belief are the two most astonishing things in the world.

I am committed to emulating Jesus Christ's example with regard to people. I want to have the same attitude toward people that Jesus had. This is my commitment, and this is my motivation. I want a heart like Jesus Christ's, and that's plainly known to be possible, even for sinners like me. God sends his Spirit to live in our hearts once we've truly believed in Jesus, for the plain and simple reason that we can't live up to his standards about love. But he can! And his Holy Spirit can make us that way too!

Jesus came down off a mountain and there was a great big crowd following him, and a leper came to him and worshiped him. Lepers were absolutely vile. They had to stand outside the city and yell "Unclean" at the top of their lungs before they could even come into town, and they had to enter on the other side of the street. Nobody touched the leper. Mark's account says he knelt down before Jesus and cried, "Lord, if you wanted to, you could make me well." And Jesus reached out and touched him, the only person in the whole civilized world that would think of touching a leper.

134

Nobody is going to hurt in the presence of Jesus. He cared about people, people that didn't matter, people you usually don't care about. A little crook wanted to see Jesus, but he was too short. There was always too big a crowd around him. So he ran down the Jericho road and climbed into a sycamore tree. Jesus passed under the tree and looked up and saw him. He didn't

say, "You little crook, this mob behind me hates your
insides. It would ruin my reputation if I associated with
you. Take a good look, 'cause I'm going by." No! He
said to the little crook, "Come on down, I'm going to
go home with you." A little extortioner, despised by the
self-righteous crowd that frequently pursued Jesus, was
offered divine companionship in the presence of the
whole bunch. Jesus never cared what somebody else
thought. He loved people. That little guy, walking by
the side of the Savior down to his house for supper, felt
nine feet tall all the way home!

And there was another crook, remember? A crook
that was fastened to a cross, a criminal, dying for his
crime. His companion in crime was also on a cross. But
on the center cross was one who was dying for people
who have trouble with crime. His lifeblood was flowing
down the old, rugged cross. And the crook turned and
said, "Lord, remember me." He had no chance to go
and make anything right. He had no chance to go and
live an ethical, godly life to prove that he meant business with Christ. Out of his misery and suffering and
guilt he simply said, "Lord, remember me." And the
dying Savior turned on his bloody cross and said to the
crook, "You're going with me, today. We'll be together
in Paradise." To a crook on a tree he offered friendship
and compassion. To a crook on a cross he offered
heaven. Jesus loved people.

135

Then there's that touching story of the woman he met
at the well. She was a messed-up person if there ever
was one. She had already divorced five husbands. It
was probably a record for those days. He didn't talk to
her about what a miserable sinner she was. He talked
to her about who God was. He didn't condemn her. He
merely mentioned the fact that there were five preced-
ing husbands, and that her present man wasn't really
her husband. She went back to town and told the
whole town, "Come on out and see this fellow who's

been talking to me." She wouldn't have done that if he had whaled her over the head for being an adulteress. Compassion means gentleness and pity and sympathy and warmth. And Jesus Christ had compassion.

Then in the eighth chapter of John, those self-righteous rascals, the Pharisees, dragged in a woman caught in the very act of adultery. And Jesus delivered her in that way that's become famous down through the ages. "The law says to stone her, so what do we do about that?" her accusers asked. Jesus' answer was, "The one who hasn't sinned, you throw the first rock." They slunk away. From the eldest to the youngest, they faded out of the picture. Then Jesus did a tender and touching thing, because he had compassion. He reached down and with his finger started making marks in the sand.

Did you ever stop and ask yourself why he did that? He had a pretty touchy situation on his hands. Why did he do that? Why, if you've been caught red-handed in some sin you don't want somebody standing you up eyeball to eyeball! It was a nice, gentle thing to do, to lean down and busy himself with his finger in the sand. He could treat her that way because he was going to die for her, and because he knew that his love would reach out and wrap itself around her heart, and she'd cling to him forever. He was the ransom payment. Payment for sin was a serious, bloody, expensive business. God never treated sin lightly, but he never roughed up sinners.

Jesus made up a story one day. He had only two characters in this story, one a good man, the other a bad man. And he made the bad man a hero! The good man went up front in the church and prayed a long-winded prayer, a ridiculous kind of prayer when you really analyze it. But the bad man, he just barely plunked into the back seat. He wasn't used to church, didn't even feel at home there. And he beat on his chest

136

and said, "God be merciful to me, a sinner." And the beautiful ending to Jesus' story is that the bad man went home all right; the poor "good" fellow was still in a box.

Jesus came to seek and to save people who are lost. So if we are going about his business in the New Testament way, then we've got to be very tender, and very gentle, and very sympathetic, and very understanding, and very loving about people that are off the track. He was, and we've got to be!

I am identified with the modern institutional church. I am a member of one of the most institutional of them all, a Presbyterian minister in good standing in my presbytery for twenty-one years. Quite a record for a fellow in my line of work. The Presbyterians frown on anything they can't control, and I'll give you a clue: they can't control me. I am identified, and I trust loyally so and constructively so, with the local, organized church. But I am also engaged in the sincere attempt to get back to what New Testament Christianity was really all about. The heart and center of it was Jesus Christ and people.

I want a chance to tell all the young people growing up in our nation about Jesus Christ and his love for them. I want to tell them in terms they can understand and appreciate. I want to tell them with their hearts and lives wide open so I know they're listening. So I simply have to emulate the example of Paul, the greatest Christian missionary, who said to be all things to all people, doing everything possible to be like they want me to be. It's a wonderful thing to have kids come every week after camp and say, "Jim, I never heard this before, or else I wasn't listening before." We take them up Chimney Rock and scare them, and we take them up the snow slides and get them frozen; we ramble around, we feed them too much, we go all out all the time to win their confidence and friendship. It's

137

no wonder that they say, "I never heard it before." No-
body ever took many pains to see that they listened be-
fore! I'll do everything to see that kids are listening.

I know so-called Christian people that the other peo-
ple in town just want to spit on. These folks have never
gone an inch out of their way for anyone. They don't
care about people. They're preaching Christ all right,
but there's something missing! I'm afraid, if the truth
were known, that most "Christians" are like that—they
never closed in with the Savior, they never were
touched by the Spirit, they never got the gospel, they
never really opened the door of their hearts—'cause
when Jesus comes into a life, he makes a difference.

Hudson Taylor went to inland China. He had a bur-
den like the burden that Paul the apostle had. He was
determined that those people farthest out were going to
hear about Jesus Christ. H. Taylor grew long hair and
wore Chinese clothes—that must have been awfully
hard for an Englishman to do. You know how stuck
the English people are; to do anything that hasn't been
done for the last 976 years would be a real trial. But he
did it for Jesus' sake, and probably H. Taylor and those
that followed H. Taylor reached more people for Jesus
Christ than anyone in modern history. Probably the
church is standing strong and true today in the midst
138 *of that Communist culture because of Hudson Taylor*
and those that followed him.

Adoniram Judson went to Burma with his heart
aflame for Jesus Christ. He was determined he was
going to reach those people for the Savior. For seven
long years he lived with those Burmese people and he
never got a convert—not one. You read the story of
how they treated him, you read of the terrible way he
suffered, you read of the way his wife died, and you'll
think impossible, foolish, ridiculous, the mission board
back home pestering him all the time to get some re-
sults, to please put some numbers on his reports. But he

kept on, and kept on living for and loving Burmese people. Finally at the end of seven years he had a convert—a little girl accepted Jesus Christ as Savior, the first Christian in Burma. The church grew strong and true, because A. Judson loved Jesus Christ and meant business about following Jesus' example.

The great Robert Moffat, father-in-law of David Livingstone, went to the Cameroons in the early days of African missions, even before Livingstone had opened up the dark continent. There in the Cameroons was a wild and vicious tribe headed by the chief, Africaner, a murderer, a brutal, sadistic savage. Moffat set his heart to reach those people, and he started with the worst one, the poorest prospect, Africaner. For years he befriended Africaner, for years he protected him from the British government, his own government. Moffat became Africaner's friend, and he became the first convert of his tribe.

So the story goes, down through Christian history. Our young people today, six or eight million in the high-school age alone, are waiting, waiting for somebody to care about them like that. I mean there are six or eight million in our nation that nobody has ever talked to about Jesus Christ, that nobody has ever said a prayer for, that nobody has ever cared about. There are millions of them in our own nation, and they are waiting for somebody to care about them enough to take the time and trouble to pour out compassion on them, to prove their friendship, to bridge this tragic and terrible gap that exists in our culture between teenagers and adults—to emulate the example of Jesus Christ. They're waiting for somebody, and I believe you and I and the people whose lives we touch have to be that somebody. I pray that we'll lift up our eyes to the multitudes, like Jesus did, 'cause a million kids is a multitude, two million is one whale of a multitude, six or eight million I can't even imagine.

It is the divine Spirit that implants such burdens into the hearts of Christ's people. Jim had awakened late to the realization that some of his people were not so "fired up," not so burdened for the task at hand as he was. He figured that theological studies might provide his staff with that same fire. He wasn't willing, however, to lose their services for three years while they studied at a seminary. As he saw it, there was only one solution—to start his own summer school. So in 1955 he formed the Young Life Institute, a graduate school, in hopes that it would lead his people to a deeper appreciation of authentic Christianity. Today Jim's school is nearly thirty years old and fully accredited. It has just been moved from Colorado Springs to Holland, Michigan.

Brad Curl, Washington, D.C. businessman and former member of Jim's staff, talks about the kind of faith Jim hoped to develop in his staff:

"Jim was calling sharp men and women to sacrifice, to risk starving to death for the purpose of reaching kids. At times, when the testings came, there wasn't any food in the cupboards. Jim was pushing his people toward the spiritual peaks, asking them to place all their needs in the hands of God. For his staff there was always the temptation to think, 'Man, there are folks out there no smarter than me, same education as I have, and they're making five times what I'm making.' Jim was calling his people to be suffering servants, to take up the cross. He knew there wasn't any other way to get the job done. He had a burden from the Spirit, and he wanted his people to feel it too.

"What we largely have today is a crossless faith. It's considered sacrilegious to ask someone to make a sacrifice for Christ. People don't want to pay the price any more—they just shout for more administration, more fund-raising techniques, higher salaries, better benefits, etc. The irony is that the sharpest young men and women, tomorrow's generation of leaders, are looking for the kind of risk-it-all commitment that Jim called his people to in the first place."

FOURTEEN
Breakdown

GOD'S adversary had thrown everything imaginable at Jim and Maxine from the moment of Jim's
spiritual breakthrough: nervous breakdowns, a ruptured appendix, attacks by the institutional church,
lightning bolts, fires, increased migraine attacks, financial problems, drug problems, and marital discord.
Throughout the fifties, these battles raged on.

Maxine had major surgery on her legs in 1949. A
hysterectomy in 1950 brought on surgical menopause.
She was back in the hospital in 1952 for another leg
operation. That same year saw further surgery on her
mouth. In 1954, a complicated surgical procedure was

performed on her feet. Two years later, it was spinal surgery, another attempt to correct the herniated disk. Beginning in 1952, she fought her own battle with migraine headaches. Discouraged by Jim's and her own failing health, Max lost the battle to control her weight. By the mid-fifties she had ballooned to over two hundred pounds. Thereafter, it was difficult to get her out of the house; feeling fat and unattractive, she lost all interest in socializing with others.

By 1954 Jim was physically, spiritually, and emotionally spent. Migraine headaches were occurring three to four days apart, and sleepless nights were commonplace. Maxine says, "Jim was totally exhausted and sinking fast. I knew he needed help. I wasn't in any position to assist him, as I was having such a struggle in my own right, but I could see he was in trouble; someone had to come to his aid. I contacted some friends who gave the money for Jim to take a world trip. He left in October and was gone for three months."

Jim desperately needed this reprieve. There were several areas of intense stress in his life. In the short span of a few years, his little "Texas experiment" had mushroomed into a sizable outreach. Jim had unintentionally created, and found himself the pastor of, a church. It was not a typical, organized, denominational church, but a twentieth-century Christian church searching for its heritage in the pages of the New Testament. It was an orphan church, a motherless child thrown into the open field (Ezek. 16:4-5). There were no buildings, no organ, no white-collared clergy, no stained-glass windows, no confessional, and precious little structure. What was called Young Life was simply a diverse, lovable group of people united under Jim's leadership by a sincere concern for kids and varying commitments to Christ. Pastoring and

144

providing leadership for this unlikely group had become a full-time job.

All the duties usually incumbent on a corporate president were Jim's, and these responsibilities alone were another full-time situation. This was the hat in Jim's closet that didn't fit very well, the one that gave him headaches, but it was the hat his board of directors most wanted him to wear. They could relate to that hat; they were familiar with it—many of them were corporate presidents as well. As with any good corporate board of directors, their main concern was financial stability. Was the ship on sound financial waters or not?

There was no way Jim could guarantee smooth sailing over calm financial seas. The challenge facing a disciple is to walk with Christ on top of the waves, to exercise faith, to believe in and trust the promptings of the Spirit within. When Peter stopped to look at the waves on which he was standing, to count the dollars in his bank account, he started to sink. Jim had learned that when his eyes were stayed on Jesus Christ, he didn't sink. The worst thing he could do was to count his money; it took his eyes off Christ.

But Jim was not a superman. At times the financial needs of his people and the financial concerns of his board rose like giant waves of pressure threatening to engulf him. Further, it drained him to be constantly doubted by his close companions. The contention surrounding him was drowning the quiet whisper of God's Spirit. The pressure was unreal, and it was utterly destroying his health.

145

The world cruise that Maxine arranged was a godsend. By trip's end, the interval between migraines had jumped to three weeks; Jim was feeling like a new man. But the pressures he had left in San Francisco were there to greet him when he docked in New

York. Excerpts from his 1955 journal show the sudden change in mood:

1/20: *Very rough sea. Read C. S. Lewis and the Word all day. Wonderful time in prayer. The improvement in my devotional life very real and important to me. Great day!*

1/21: *Studied his Word and had prayerful meditation this whole day. A great day!*

1/22: *One of the greatest days in prayer and the Word I've ever had. Especially remembered my home, loved ones, and fellow workers.*

1/23: *Another grand day of worship. Having fun remembering the great days of skiing at Davos and Zermatt. What a sport! The greatest ski runs I ever saw— and faster. A wonderful day, a wonderful trip. Best of all has been the time in prayer, meditation, and study. It's the best I've had in years.*

1/24: *Arrived New York this morning. Norm and Eastern staff greeted me. A hard, lonesome day.*

1/25: *To Chicago for board of directors meeting tomorrow. Migraine—first one of the year.*

146 1/26: *Board meeting today. I wish I hadn't come. Could just as well have gone home for all the good it did. Am very disappointed, and discouraged, about the condition of the work. But that means the Lord must take a larger place with me. His will is all that matters.*

Administrative details, management hassles, fundraising duties, board meetings, committee meetings, and demanding schedules all triggered long runs of vicious migraines. God does not call people to self-destruction; it is difficult to believe that these activities were a necessary part of Jim's "calling." He was a spiritual leader, not a corporate executive.

Jim gave little emphasis to job descriptions, personnel files, organizational charts, policy formulation, and so on. As his outfit continued to grow, however, his administrative deficiencies mushroomed into a sizable problem. Jim's board, deeply concerned by the situation, adopted an "Organization Plan" in January 1957. Under the guise of relieving Jim of administrative concerns, this plan specified new lines of authority, a new organizational structure, specific job descriptions, and "effective programs of financial planning and budgetary control."

This new plan, however well intentioned, was the genesis of a tragedy, as it called for Jim's staff to become heavily involved in administration and management. Jim wished his staff to be freed from these distractions. As he viewed it: *God has given us a great and holy task. I cannot think of any area of the church's activity more critical than the one we (Young Life leaders) face everyday. We desperately need adult committee people, people who are wise and full of God's Spirit, to handle the business end of things, to build the platform of support upon which the Young Life leader stands. But here is where we have to stand—we will give ourselves continually to prayer, and to sharing Christ with the high-school crowd. And that's all! Committee people must do their task so that we may do ours. That's where we have to stand—given only to the ministry of God's Word, and prayer.*

In 1956 a medical doctor from Washington prescribed for Jim a new wonder drug—Dexamyl, a strong amphetamine. It was guaranteed to pick him up, make him feel better, and possibly help the headache situation. Jim's initial prescription was a "small" one—only one thousand capsules! Almost instantly, the

147

new drug had a marvelous effect; Jim's health and energy level soared to new heights and remained there for several years.

But by the early sixties Jim was beginning to experience adverse reactions to the drug: severe stomach disorders, short periods of confusion, mild tremors, irritability, and intense fatigue. All are symptoms of amphetamine poisoning. Tragically, Jim's doctors continued to supply him with these drugs. The long-range effects were devastating.

Dexamyl, a strong amphetamine, is now known to cause marked insomnia, irritability, hyperactivity, and personality changes. Dizziness, tremors, headaches, dryness of mouth, diarrhea, various gastrointestinal disturbances, and even psychotic episodes are other adverse reactions. At one time or another, Jim experienced every one of these symptoms. No one suspected the cause.

Eventually drug-induced gastrointestinal disturbances led to stomach surgery in June of 1961. This was the coup de grâce to Jim's elusive moments of good health. The nerve controlling the quantity of digestive juices to the stomach was severed, and over half of his stomach was removed. It was a rare day thereafter when he could digest food normally. A process known as "dumping," in which the stomach empties its contents into the small intestine without performing any digestive function, caused him many problems throughout the sixties. The following entry in his diary for 1961 is typical:

148

11/16: *A wonderful time of prayer/meditation early this morning, in spite of sleepless night. So weary I can hardly stand or see. Arrived in Philadelphia too "pooped" to do anything. Exhausted beyond endurance and just about sick. Not sleeping well lately. The "dumping" hits me frequently and I am too uncomfort-*

able for sleep. Finished day with an unparalleled time of prayer. The degree of concentration was seemingly higher than any I've achieved—the enormous range of subjects and people that the Spirit brought to my attention was amazing—and the requests made for individual people. . . . Am so thankful for the outpouring of his Spirit, and this special measure of his enabling grace.

The downhill course of Jim's health runs in strange contrast to the ever blossoming longings in his heart. In a sense, the man had not yet started to dream.

FIFTEEN
Visions and Controversy

WITH increased international exposure in the
late fifties and early sixties, Jim had become . . . cosmopolitan. . . . His compassion for kids was now
focused on all the world's teenagers. Although he visited, and stayed in, some of the worst ghettos known,
he frequently rubbed shoulders with the world's rich-
est and most politically powerful people as well.
Whether he was sleeping in a mud hut in Africa or a
palace in Europe, Jim's warmth, personality, and sa-
voir-faire made him equally at home with people of
high station and of low.

Jim had a sensitivity to other cultures that would

put most diplomats to shame. Long before terms such as *global community* became fashionable, he viewed the world as a global village. He had the feel of life as experienced by the poorest of the poor—in Pakistan, India, Africa, the American Indian reservations, and the hinterlands of South America. There were few places Jim hadn't been and no group of people he didn't love. Indeed, his heart was filled with the divine Spirit that looks upon the multitude and feels compassion.

In a world that prefers black-robed and white-collared clergy, Jim was far too cosmopolitan for some people's tastes. He not only knew which wine he preferred, he knew the vintage. In the company of intellectuals who preferred conversation about Plato, Socrates, Kant, or Hegel, Jim was always well versed and eager for conversation. I can still remember his saying in that deep, slow, Jimmy Stewart drawl, "Why, those European kids always want to talk to me about existentialism; these kids here in the United States don't even know what the word means. All they want to talk about is last year's football team, or this year's cheerleading squad. Why, it makes one wonder what's wrong with our educational system."

For all his depth, Jim's ever-present sense of humor would bubble to the surface on any occasion. In reporting on a trip abroad to a rather large and conservative church, Jim injected, "Why, the carpets on that ship were so plush, I ran around all day without my pants on, and nobody knew the difference." Only a sourpuss by nature could fail to like Jim; he was too sincere, too real, too funny, and too warm to resist.

In the spring of 1959, Jim had his first exposure to East Berlin. It was an experience that changed his life. Horrified by what he'd seen of life under Communist rule, Jim vowed to fight back. A maturing and deepening earnestness about his work gave birth to a new

singleminded purpose: to build God's kingdom before
he lost the opportunity.

Wasting no time, Jim took eleven of his men to Europe in November 1959. For most, it was their first exposure to foreign shores. Jim felt like a father taking
his boys out to dine at their first gourmet restaurant.
Journal excerpts tell the story.

11/13: *A restful day. The food is wonderful, and the sea
is unbelievably calm. I think my boys are getting a big
kick out of it. The ship and service are perfect in every·
way. The boys sure looked swell "dressed" for dinner.*

11/22: *To East Berlin with the whole crowd this afternoon. A powerful experience. I'll never forget the nine-
teen-year-old's moving prayer, "We'll never again see
each other here . . . only in the kingdom."*

11/24: *Where but in Berlin could one have such a
heartsearching experience? We went to the Marienfelds
Reception Center this morning. Sat in on a "trial" of
young East German who has tried for two years to
reach his wife in the West—has given up everything.
Some wonderful time with dozens of little kindergarten
kids—they call me "Uncle Jim." Interviewed a nineteen-
year-old girl who just escaped from Leipzig. Great to
be with Bill, Tim, and Orien.*

11/25: *An hour with Mayor Willy Brandt this morning.
Also had a great experience in a teenage boys' camp—
about two hundred boys who'd escaped to the West
after their parents "mysteriously disappeared." Grand
and shocking case histories by personal account.*

153

It frightened Jim to see that most Communist revo-
lutionaries are more dedicated to world change than
Christians are. By exposing his men to the horrors of
Soviet Communism, Jim hoped to raise the level of

their concern. He told a high-school assembly about his discoveries in East Germany:

People tell me, "That's all right, Jim; they're over there and we're over here. It's not our problem." But anybody who says that is not only a traitor to a free way of life, he's a traitor to the human race.

Berlin is a little island of freedom in a sea of slavery. To walk from freedom into horror, you only have to cross the street. With my heart in my mouth, I took my daughter's hand and walked across that line. I wondered if we'd ever get back. We hadn't walked ten feet before we felt the difference. Not a single person smiled; we could smell the fear in the people. Not one single person on the streets dared to greet us. Fear permeates the atmosphere.

We met East Berlin University kids and lots of high-school kids, and they all told us the same thing, "We can't go where we want to; we can't say what we want to; we can't get together in groups; we can't go to church; we can't study what we want to."

I thought, "Surely this can't be true in the world we live in today, and it surely can't be true that people will sit idly by and not do anything for all the folks who are suffering under this dehumanizing system of government."

154

Jim's convictions were deepening. The weight of suffering humanity was tearing at his heart. He was a man with a burden, a heavenly compassion implanted within by the Holy Spirit of God. There was no escaping the heart-wrenching memory of smileless faces and empty eyes behind the Iron Curtain. Nor could Jim turn his back on the desperate need of the world's teenagers, so many of whom do not have an adult friend who truly cares about them.

These deep concerns gave birth to another miracle.

He had dreamed for years of building a lodge for
adults, a glorified Lookout, from which he could share
the burdens of his heart with a large number of
guests at one time.

I first became aware of Jim's plan while hiking with
him on the slopes of Mt. Harvard, just outside Buena
Vista, Colorado. As we sat to rest on a large boulder,
high atop a gorgeous ridge, he told me of his dream.
Right where we were sitting he wanted to build his
fantasy facility, a first-class resort to rival any hotel in
the country. And from that place he planned to share
his life, his God, and his burdens with as many people
as were led to him.

It was a glorious dream, but most of his people had
little enthusiasm for such a preposterous idea. The
problem, they thought, was finding the money to pay
for such a project.

Jim's board of directors was an unusually affluent
group; most were high-powered, successful businessmen. By and large, these men were not used to being
followers or taking orders; in the business world, their
word was law. In Young Life, however, Jim's word
was law, and several on the board of directors re-
sented his strong leadership style. Jim was rapidly becoming the number-one target in a deadly serious
power struggle.

155

A board member recalls: "When Jim would give his
director's report we would sit there awestruck by the
quality and imagination of the man. He was phenomenal! But as we got into the fiscal responsibility, or a
judgment decision on economics, we were just torn
apart as businessmen. There was such a gap between
following Jim's leadership on the one hand and handling the economics to keep up with him on the other.
At almost every board meeting we had to make the
choice of following Jim or closing him out."

One of Jim's former staff analyzes the problem: "It's

very unsettling for people who are close to someone like Jim—you know, a man who will grab his buddies and go sit on a mountaintop to pray all night! People like Jim who are called to do that have to do it, whether the people around them understand or not. It would have been easier on Jim if he'd been surrounded by more people who understood, but that's not the point. One who's anointed can't afford to dwell upon that.

"There were fine, responsible people around Jim who were deeply challenged, if not upset, by his abandon to the great spiritual heights. They wanted to go along with him, but were struggling with the cost of doing so. People don't go easily into that ecstatic, joyous, costly, cross-bearing experience; they kick and scream a lot along the way. Whenever someone reaches for the heights like Jim did, he becomes such a threat! Usually, such a person has to pay the price for that; Jim certainly did."

As the tumultuous sixties arrived, Jim found himself embroiled in controversy. He was pushing a most unpopular adult lodge project, committed to the international expansion of his mission, battling a reluctant board of directors, and lashing out publicly against the organized church, as in this talk:

Three years ago Bishop Russell Hubbard asked me what I'd do with the incredible problem in the organized church—to make the church be in touch with the secular community. Well, I was in the company of a dear friend, so I felt the freedom to speak my mind.

I told the bishop that I'd like to scrap about everything the church does, that we'd have to stop doing what we're doing and start over. I'd certainly scuttle the Sunday-school programs, in their present form, because kids over twelve years of age hate it. One can't teach about Christ in an environment that people hate.

*My idea is that Sunday school will have to be neither
Sunday, nor school.*

*Kids can't wait until Friday afternoon when they can
bust out of school for the weekend! So what do we
Christians do? We insist they go back to school on Sunday morning! Of all the silly notions I ever heard, that
one about tops the list! And I'd sure enough scuttle the
evening youth group. That one has got to go!*

*I have some wonderful ideas concerning what you
could do with a morning worship service. I believe
there are forty-eight known ways, and forty-eight thousand unknown ways, to have a time that would be creative, attractive, and help people's hearts flow out to
God, which is just what worship is supposed to do.
True worship almost never happens in church.*

*You go to church to worship, but you get bombarded
with a lousy choir, or some soprano who is louder
than the whole bass section. You go away determined
that you've worshiped, but in your innermost heart,
you know you haven't. You just got nauseated by the
soprano. Why, there's been almost no creative effort in
worship service since the Vikings discovered Labrador.*

*There's no evidence in the Bible that any New Testa-
ment church acted remotely like we act! I can't understand such foolishness! One of the things that gripes me
is that a fourth of many services is taken to announce
the extra-curricular activities. I wonder how much time
the Apostle Paul spent telling about the men's club Friday evening fish fry? For goodness sake, where did we
get so far off the ball? We act like we don't even know
what Jesus Christ, the gospel, and the Christian life is
about.*

*I go to church, although I'm not sure why, sit
through the whole dull business, and go on home figur-
ing I'll bore myself silly for an hour the next Sunday
repeating the whole ritual. Pastors have told me that
they know this isn't right, but they don't know what to*

157

do about it. Just recently, a pastor of one of the largest churches in the country told me, with tears in his eyes, that he doubted if there was one true (born of the Spirit) Christian in his congregation. And he has four thousand members!

The institutional church has brought us such a messed-up type of "Christianity," there's no justification in even calling it by that name. When will the church start doing true church work, and stop considering ushering, and passing the collection plate, church work? If there's anything that's truly ridiculous, it's what we call church work! You can be the most active guy in church, and make a list of all the things you do: count the money, participate in clean-up day, usher, sponsor the youth group, and so on, but by the standards of the New Testament, not one thing on your list is church work. Not a thing! Church work is done out in society.

Christ is the strongest, grandest, most attractive personality ever to grace the earth. But a careless messenger with the wrong approach can reduce all this magnificence to the level of boredom. . . . It is a crime to bore anyone with the gospel!

Many of Jim's dearest friends were important leaders in the institutional churches; they understood what he was saying and agreed with it. But they too were men of the Spirit. There were other people in Jim's orbit who took offense at such a strong negative stance toward organized religion. After all, Jim had once seemed to be a staunch ally of the organized church, and now he apparently had no use for it. One thing is certain—Jim had rattled the wrong cage.

158

SIXTEEN

Exile

JIM wasn't simply respected by his people; in some ways he was idolized. Four who worked with him recall their impressions:

> I was on Jim's staff in the early fifties. I didn't know him well, as I was young and somewhat intimidated by such a great man. I'd heard a lot of people pray, but when I heard Jim pray, I knew that everything I'd heard before was suspect. I was awed; when I'd hear him talk to God, I felt that I was standing before God, too.

I've never met a person with so much charisma. He reminded me very much of Will Rogers. His effect on people was powerful, which gave him an influence I'm not sure he fully grasped. And that frightened me some. Had the human side of Jim taken over, he could have led us anywhere. He was an amazing man; I think most of us would have followed him to the edge of hell.

As a speaker, he was the best I ever heard. I'd laugh so hard I'd feel drained, and then I'd weep as Jim took us to the feet of Jesus Christ. He could have led us in so many directions, but he always took us to Jesus Christ. Many of us, however, were following Jim, and he was following Christ. We didn't have that same intimacy with God that he knew.

Jim was a man's man, a man with courage, a man with guts, a man who'd lay his life on the line for what he believed. I've never met a person with so many God-given gifts. Had he permitted it, most of us would have worshiped him. Some did, I believe, and that was a cause of much hurt. After years of careful thought I've come to my own conclusion— God gave Jim a healthy dosage of "frailties of the flesh" to help him. The spiritual side of Jim, the man with the power, was so tremendous that there needed to be human weaknesses to help him avoid being idolized.

160

Jim had seemed invincible, indestructible, almost awesome in his abilities and charisma. There seemed to be no problem big enough to defeat the man. He had led his people into the wilderness, passed through a "Red Sea" or two, and conquered the land. He had made Christ a living reality to thousands, pioneered a fresh, live movement within a stagnant religious system, scattered disciples throughout the world, and taught his people the meaning of prayer, faith, and dedication. But in the end, he showed them his humanity.

As the tumultuous sixties rolled around, things collapsed on Jim. His cross had been heavy, and he'd carried it a lot of miles. Since October 27, 1937, the day something snapped inside the pretty young girl he'd married, life had been a difficult road. A quarter century had passed and Jim still lacked a solution. Maxine remained a crippled victim of narcotics. Finding a solution seemed hopeless, and Jim was near the end of his rope.

Unable to sleep well, digest food properly, or decrease the migraine attacks, Jim turned to sleeping pills to help him rest. His stomach seldom dissolved the pills when they were needed. At numerous public appearances his speech was slurred and his message disoriented. On one such occasion in a leading Methodist church, he could not speak at all. In front of a packed house, Jim rose to speak and could not do so; he began to weep, turned to take his seat, and collapsed.

As word of these public failures spread, feelings of anger, confusion, and doubt rose to the surface throughout Young Life. "What's happening to Rayburn? How could he do such a thing?" "Is our leader drinking or turning to drugs?" All eyes focused on "the Boss." In the eyes of some, the beloved and much respected leader had fallen into sin. Sadly, there was far more anger than compassion.

Jim had understood his staff's devotion as love, not realizing that for some he was a father figure, for others a hero, and for others a spiritual giant who could do no wrong. He was emotionally and professionally vulnerable to his flock, and he never dreamed that his co-laborers would refuse to follow him. But Jim had never seen himself through the eyes of his people. It would have frightened him had he done so.

Some of those in Jim's family of followers had committed their lives to him, placed him on a pedestal demanding near perfection, and put their faith in his faith. When the leader fell from their pedestal, the flock was confused and angry. It was said by some that he was not the inspired leader he'd once been, that God had withdrawn his anointing. Further, Jim had stirred up a hornets' nest with his comments on institutionalized Christianity. "When Jim took on the institutional churches, he signed his death warrant," a staff member says. "There were not enough of his people who understood where he was coming from. They had to get him out, and his failing health gave them the opportunity." Some felt an immediate need to silence him, lest the corporation offend numerous donors.

In this atmosphere of internal turmoil, Jim rammed his adult lodge project past a reluctant board of directors. In so doing, he sealed his fate. Says a staff member: "There's no question in my mind that Jim's adult lodge was the coup de grâce as far as the board of directors was concerned. The argument put forth was that a sane mind could not have conceived such a project." With financial demands mounting throughout the mission, there was far more fear than faith among Jim's board members. A Young Life board member recalls:

"For years we had sat there and let Jim's leadership supersede the economic problems we had. Our respect for him and his love for the Savior was greater than our insistence that the mission be sensibly plotted out from an economic perspective. We kind of relaxed and figured, 'Well, maybe a mission doesn't have to be run like a business, even though it gives us some problems.' Eventually, we figured we'd have to close Jim out."

Some of the pain in this tragic episode might have
been avoided had Jim been less rigid. But he had
largely ignored requests that he delegate more authority or voluntarily accept a lesser position. By not
heeding their advice, Jim had offended several members of his board; anger replaced wisdom, and frustra-
tion took the place of compassion.

A staff member analyzes the situation:

> "There's a pattern in history that shows us that
> men will start new movements to address the
> changing needs of the world. Then, bureaucrats
> come in and build an institution. That institution,
> born to express life, then begins to stifle life.
> Whenever we get to the place of saying, 'Wait a
> minute, we don't want to sacrifice anymore—we
> want retirement benefits, better fund-raising tech-
> niques, more administration—we want this thing
> run like I.B.M.' When we get to that point, we lose
> the guts of the cross, we lose the adventure, and
> we lose the vitality of the faith.
>
> "Jim's board and staff had a tiger by the tail—he
> wasn't about to change his whole approach when
> he felt that God was leading him in other direc-
> tions. Jim would say, 'I've got the board down my
> neck, and my staff is three months behind in sal-
> ary, but I'm not stopping. We're not put here to sit
> around and atrophy. There are kids in Europe,
> Asia, Africa, and South America with virtually no
> chance to hear about Christ as they should, so
> that's where we're going.' Jim was committed to
> international expansion; his people weren't. Jim
> was building Trail West Lodge; his people didn't
> want it. Jim was telling the institutional churches
> what they needed to hear, but rocking a lot of
> boats in the process. So, they kicked him out; if
> that doesn't follow the historical norm, then I
> don't know much about history."

A seemingly well-conceived and carefully planned movement was launched to remove Jim from power. Exactly who initiated it and where it began is known only to God and those involved. Strict secrecy was maintained until the hour came to strike. Maxine observes: "I have always felt that when a person is limping and needs help, there's only one response to the situation—to provide whatever help you're able to. Jim was obviously in need of love and support from his family and associates, and in this critical hour of opportunity a movement was launched to remove him from everything he'd sacrificed so much to build. I was an eyewitness to the suffering this dear man went through; I had caused a lot of it over the years, and I honestly believe it would have been more humane had Jim been taken out and shot. I don't say that in a bitter or angry way—I just feel it would have been more honest and it would have saved Jim years of untold suffering."

On May 5, 1964, Jim was called to Chicago to meet with certain members of his board of directors. Jim's journal: *Another full day at office with the advisory committee [top level staff men]. Received call from two board members; I'm to meet them in Chicago Saturday. Sounded grim. I talked to my men about this—they gave their unanimous assurance that they want me in my customary office—will back me, etc.*

A member of that Advisory Committee who was in Jim's office when the board members called says: "That whole nightmare is almost too painful for me to talk about, so I'll say this once and hope I never have to talk about it again. Jim knew that something was up when he received that call from Chicago. As I recall, everyone present that day gave Jim his verbal assurance of support—within the next ten days, we were voting on a successor. With exception of George Sheffer, I can't recall that anyone supported Jim when the

rubber met the road. Jim must have felt completely
betrayed."

Even Jim's plane ride to Chicago was an ominous
preview of events to follow. He wrote in his journal:
*Worked hard at the office this morning. Left for Chi-
cago at 2:00 p.m. That was the roughest trip I ever
made in a plane—through severe thunder showers and
extreme turbulence—drinks and lunch trays were
thrown all over—a real mess!*

The ax fell on Saturday. By the next week, Jim was
already an outsider. He wrote:

5/8: *This was an unbelievable night. I left this shocking, late night, futile conversation, virtually in a state
of shock! I'm to be stripped of all authority, and begin
a one-year sabbatical leave in August. Start summer as
usual, but keep out of program and fade out of the picture by July 1st. Are these men qualified? Is there vision
on the board? It seems, except for a few individuals, to
have always been lacking.*

5/12: *Called a meeting of my advisory committee in
Denver. The same board members included themselves
without communicating with me.*

*Either tonight or in the morning the advisory com-
mittee convened without me, the board men taking
over. They are not members of this committee and have
no authorization to call it together. What is happening?
IMPOSSIBLE!*

The minutes of the national board of directors
meeting, held at Franklin Park, Illinois, on June 3-5,
1964, show the board's thinking. Here is an excerpt:

> Mr. Hull inquired whether the whole matter of
> Jim's removal had come up suddenly. He said he
> had been concerned for some time over Jim's

physical condition, but that Jim now appeared to him to be a man without hope. He cautioned the group not to walk ahead of God. Mr. "X" said the purpose of the May 12 meeting in Denver was to clarify matters of Jim's health and administrative capability. The meeting was called by Jim, but Mr. "X" and Mr. "Y" requested a hearing since it dealt with the perpetuity in office of the executive director.

Several questions immediately arise: Who informed these members of Jim's board that he had called a meeting of his staff advisers? What moral or legal right did these men have to usurp Jim's meeting? As Jim was the only one who could grant a hearing, why had such a request not come directly to him? As Jim had been told on May 8th that he was soon to be fired, why were many members of his board unaware of any such action?

A close friend of Jim and Maxine says: "I was at those Denver meetings and came away deeply disturbed. First of all, the board men who were there had no right to be, in my eyes—it was Jim's meeting and they took control of it. What bothered me most, however, was the talk about Jim that took place behind closed doors. It wasn't honoring to Jim, and it most certainly wasn't honoring to Christ."

Jim's journal continues the story: *Executive committee of the board (with advisory committee called in from time to time) met for an hour and a half* without my being able to find them. *Finally I got with them and couldn't believe what was happening. I left this afternoon crushed—no one came to me! This seems now to have been the darkest day of my life. I must hang onto the Lord—"I will never leave thee nor forsake thee" is for me too.*

On June 3 Jim was in Illinois for the board of direc-

166

tors meeting. His journal records: *I read my statement to the board, then left. Not in all the last four terrible weeks has an executive committee member spoken to me alone. I must correct this before I give way. Dear Jesus, what have we come to?*

The following morning, the board reconvened without Jim present. The discussion centered largely on Jim's mental health, the implication being that he was a very sick man. After lengthy discussion, it was decided to give him a token title and a promise that he could return to the work if he would submit to psychiatric treatment. Jim wrote: *I was brought into the board meeting, after an all morning wait, and was told the executive committee had recommended that I keep my title of executive director, although on leave and with no authority. It's obvious to me that they plan to superannuate me at the end of the year.*

The shock to Jim was real. The negative spirit in the air was a clear indication of the Holy Spirit's absence, and Jim was deeply concerned for his life's work. There is nothing more agonizing to a man of integrity than to find that the best people leave him alone, not because they are unaware of his suffering, but because they doubt his word. With the sudden disappearance of his most faithful supporters, Jim was left alone with God.

167

During this stormy board meeting, Mr. John Carter questioned the wisdom of removing Jim permanently. Mr. "X" responded "that the essence of the original intent was that the change be permanent." Later, Mr. Hull asked if the board really did want Jim back, provided his health improved. Mr. "Z" snapped, "Back as what?" He said Jim hadn't demonstrated administrative talent.

Jim knew he'd never be asked to return, that references to a "leave of absence" were nothing more than a placebo. Jim was passing through the darkest valley of his life, while the board was issuing its final resolution:

> At the conclusion of this resolution, we reaffirm
> our pledge to pray for and work for Jim's complete recovery; praising God (as we pray) for what
> he has accomplished through Jim as founder and
> leader of Young Life from its earliest days to the
> present; and knowing that God has yet greater
> things for his people, praying with faith and hope,
> with trust and confidence, that Jim's body, soul,
> and spirit will be in health and prosper; and that
> he will go from strength to strength and be even
> more fruitful in this work in future days.

The Board agreed to allow Jim and his family one
more summer's residence at his much loved Lookout
at Frontier Ranch. The project that had cost him so
much, Trail West Lodge, was only ten miles away, and
it had just opened its doors for the first summer of operation. Jim's emotions lifted some when the national
conference for Young Life committeemen opened at
this beautiful facility on July 20, 1964. The very next
day, however, Jim was ordered out of Trail West,
given a directive to pack his family and leave the
Lookout, and told he was not to set foot on any Young
Life-owned property again. He was given less than
twenty-four hours to comply.

It seemed appropriate that when the news of our
eviction arrived, Goldbrick and Jerry were there to
share our tears and help us pack. Together they recall: "Things were never the same after that. When
we saw that happening to Jim, we knew that we, or
anybody else, could get the same treatment. It was not
a happy time. That was the day a family became an
organization."

As the full extent of his exile began to dawn upon
him, Jim's emotions broke down. Within months, the

man's health was at an all-time low; he was visibly suffering, slowly dying from a broken heart. In early August, his two sons-in-law visited him in Colorado Springs. Jim wanted them to see the new headquarters building of which he'd been proud, so he sent them over with his key, as he was not allowed to go himself. *That's when I found out they had changed all the locks so that I couldn't get into the building. This was a very low time for me—the ultimate humiliation.*

The impossible continued. Jim's confidential files (sacred ground to ministers, doctors, lawyers, and other professionals) were searched, and members of his family were forbidden to set foot on any Young Life property for as long as they lived. Before long, most of his friends stopped calling, and old acquaintances acted nervous, cool, and aloof in Jim's presence. He knew his friends had heard something, but that was all he knew.

To be wounded by your friends takes you by surprise; it is a bitter pill. But Jim had prayed to share in the suffering of Christ; now the hour had arrived. Within a few months, he had gone from being one of the most respected Christian leaders on the world scene to being a discredited, much maligned shadow of a human being; his health had gone from bad to disastrous. He was in a state of despair, the hopelessness that overtakes a sane mind when it is pushed to the extreme in grief. Jim wrote in his journal:

169

9/28: *Had a fine time with my "Doc." He asked me to think about why I'm not suspicious about people, and why I don't realize that otherwise good people are capable of plotting against me. He said I was to think it over, that I'm naive.*

10/2: *The day of inexplicable terror! Had breakfast with Lanes, haircut, and then the big trouble. I was still shaking and perspiring so that I could hardly talk*

*to my doctor, but glad he could see me in that state.
The only thing of this kind I have ever experienced, a
living hell.*

*10/28: A bad day, except for some good, though brief,
time in prayer. When, O Lord, when will come the end
of this, and how shall I speed the day—while ever trust-
ing you?*

Although removed from the Young Life board of directors at the June meeting, Jim could scarcely believe he wouldn't be asked back. The next meeting
was scheduled for November 12 in Dallas, and Jim ex-
pectantly awaited an invitation that never came. His
journal takes us to the end of 1964:

*11/11: A busy day in Chicago. I kept hoping I'd be
called to Dallas. Two good hours of prayer in early
morning. Life is rough for me in these, the darkest of
my days.*

*11/12: Another day—sitting on the forlorn hope—not
sure I can stand much more of this. Oh, merciful
Father . . .*

*11/23: This is the best day I've had since that terrible
knockout blow on May 8th night. Am angry again for
the first time in months.*

*11/24: This was a great day! Peace and actual happi-
ness. I had one and a half hours alone with the Lord in
a very rich time, and a grand talk about it with Maxine. Haven't had prayer like that in two years!
My doc told me he doesn't think I'm sick. Neither do
I! A wonderful day. Glory to God.*

*11/25: Tired but happy—and all my confidence is in the
Lord, as much as is in me! Put more capacity for trust-
ing you in me, Lord Jesus!*

I'm feeding upon the Scriptures—devouring passages. It must be the joy of the Lord again, as so often in the good old days— before May 8th. May 8th is my May Day.

11/26: *For third day straight I got into the Word for some rich stuff. Prayer the same—it is like the old times, say ten to fifteen years ago. The Lord God has laid his hand upon me. I am beset behind and before, but the old things are new. It cannot but come right!*

12/4: *We are immersed in beauty, but our vision is not clear. A good day with my doctor. He says they call me liberal—radical—a boat rocker.*

I wonder why not one board member gave me personal counseling regarding what I call "charges against me?" The erosion of power having once begun develops a momentum of its own. In light of recent experiences, I fear for the future of Young Life.

12/31: *What a very, very difficult year is closing. My constant prayer—Oh God of loving kindness and tender mercy—may there not be another so bad—by thy Grace, may 1965 be a wonderful year—made so by remembering, "Lo, I am with you* always." *With thy enabling grace may I find, do, and be the will of God— and truly* love *my brothers, and all men.*

171

SEVENTEEN

Into all the World

JIM'S vision had been to reach the world's young adults, the next generation, with the glorious message that God's Spirit can be known personally and that the "secret" of this discovery can be found in the birth, life, death, and resurrection of Jesus Christ. And Jim's last years were devoted to that calling.

He looked at it like this—if God's Spirit can be personally known, then what on earth could possibly be as important as that? If the claims of Christianity are true, then mankind really has something to celebrate! If the big, undefinable, awesome, beautiful, creative Spirit-Source behind this unfathomable universe has really made it possible for us humans to commune with him, then we've all got something to sing about, shout about, and put on our dancin' shoes about. There ought to be one grandiose news special coming on right now.... We interrupt this program for this special announcement—

> *God has appeared . . .*
> *He was beautiful . . .*
> *We killed him . . .*
> *He rose . . .*
> *His Spirit is alive and eternal . . .*
> *He needs a new body for his earth*
> *purposes . . .*
> *You're it!*

That's a news story worth the air time!

Jim didn't just think that story was true; he didn't just hope it was true, and he didn't just believe it was true—he knew it was true! He'd had a spiritual "eyeball to eyeball" with Jesus Christ; he had gazed into the eyes of love, and the divine Spirit had enlivened his own. He knew that Christ is risen; the story is true! Getting the word out to precious kids before their open, unspoiled minds would close was Jim's burden, cause, and purpose. In his eyes, there wasn't any other job. His was the only game in town.

Now, almost overnight, Jim found himself with no office, no people, no reputation, no secretary, poor health, and precious little money.

He felt like a man whose children had shipped him off to a home for the aging, saying dear ol' Dad was "over the hill," no longer an inspired leader, and no longer of much benefit to them. Far better to be rid of him, put him out of sight and out of mind, lest his condition be an embarrassment to all.

In a letter to Jim's board of directors, one of his psychiatrists clearly stated that the actions of that body were detrimental to Jim's health and that continuation of such treatment could, and probably would, lead to his death. This letter was virtually ignored. Board members said that the doctor was incompetent and that Jim had shrunk the shrink.

For five years we in Jim's family tried to arrange a desk for him at the Young Life headquarters. We felt that such a move might make him feel more a part of his life's work. We requested a small area in the basement with a cement floor. But there was no room in the "inn" for Jim. Unofficially, people worried that he'd try to take over once again, but no official response was ever forthcoming.

The following journal excerpts from 1967 and 1968 echo the pain of these years:

7/30: *I'm so confused, despondent, unable to pull myself together. Sometimes it's almost like strangling. I must get some "air" or I'll die. And yet I don't—and the succession of near worthless days continues . . .*

4/28: *A most difficult and almost desperate day. What reason? Couldn't study or rest, and found no satisfaction in reading. Gloomy, near to despairing—feel that I am "dying of creeping despair." And how long has this been so, but for brief intervals? Almost four years now.*

I talk to the Lord about it. Before God I feel ashamed—"my times are in his hands." He has made me know that I want his will above all else . . . and yet this repeated, perennial falling into such despondency. Oh, why?

8/5: *Maybe the worst day of my life—this morning in family room—struggling to tell Maxine that I wouldn't make it—no time left—oh, merciful Father, how much more will you allow?*

11/29: *Being "out of my job," not knowing what to do,
or how to reach those dear kids throughout the
world—it's all so very hard on me. The isolation, and
being ostracized by my long-time co-laborers and
friends, is the hardest thing to take. Am keeping it all
before the Lord, as best I know how—but my heart
seems shattered into pieces. Doubt that I have much
time left—don't know how to live this way, but don't
know how to die . . .*

Jim's early success in working with adolescents had
catapulted him to fame and power. He'd spent many
years in the spotlight, heard much applause, and
gained a fair share of approval, but in the end he did
his work alone, as he had in the beginning. There had
been no applause greeting him and Maxine in Chama,
New Mexico, and there would be no public recogni-
tion for loving kids in San Juan, Argentina; Karachi,
Pakistan; or Campinas, Brazil. But Jim felt he had a
job to do, broken heart or no, and he gave himself to
that endeavor with a fullness of purpose that tran-
scends human understanding.

By this time Jim had made friends with kids in Nor-
way, Sweden, Germany, France, Turkey, Pakistan, Ma-
laysia, India, East Germany, Argentina, Peru, Japan,
176   Brazil, and several countries in Africa. He conceived
and raised money for a beautiful kids' resort in Brazil;
a follower, Diether Koerner, was working for him full-
time in Peru; and a solid nucleus of twenty college
kids in Argentina adored him. In 1968, hoping to move
to Argentina, he took a crash course in Spanish at the
Thunderbird School in Phoenix, Arizona.

I walked with Jim in some remote parts of this
world, saw his compassion and concern for people,
and felt the sincerity of his heart. He was a man cut
from the same mold as the apostle Paul, a man with a

light in his eyes, a man touched by the Holy Spirit.
There was no river too wide to cross, no mountain too
high to climb, and no village too remote to reach. He
feared no language barrier.

His journals show the extent of his travels and the
depth of his concern:

Pakistan—*To Khyber Pass this morning. Had the most
wonderful heart-to-heart talk about the Lord and the
faith for three hours tonight—alone with Ibo. Was
worth the whole trip. How greatly he needs me, he has
"no one else to talk to." How I long for and pray . . .*

Pakistan—*Another heart-searching talk with Ibo
through the night. I must get all people I know who
really pray to remember this dear kid and his family.
To bed late—weary, thankful, deeply affected, and so
anxious to know what we can do for kids in these dark
lands. I cannot just act like they aren't there.*

Turkey—*I'm nearly cracking up because of the
farewells—how amazing, surprising, and warming to
be so needed and wanted by these dear kids. It is the
same with all.*

Sweden—*Am so concerned for the kids here. They are
all pretty well stranded—don't know any "alive" Christians. Another special stop in terms of friendship and
expressing my sincere desire to help them.*

177

Argentina—*About 9:00 p.m., in very isolated country,
we got stuck. The worst situation I ever saw. Water
was running into the car. An hour or two later five
swell guys going fishing stopped to help. They got stuck
too. Eventually, we were all out and rolling again.
Then an hour filling in a washout. Had crackers for
dinner. We are eight hundred kilometers south of San
Juan—perhaps the most beautiful country I've ever*

*seen—even prettier than Malibu. Found a peninsula
that beats anything I've seen—what a place for a kids'
resort. My head is swimming with plans for Argentina.*

Brazil—*Such attractive kids here. Met tonight with
twenty-four of them—a small number but what a far
cry from several years ago. What to do? How to get
leaders? Why doesn't anyone want to go to them? The
camp is beautiful—there's nothing like it in Latin America. The burden of Christ for these precious young lives
is on my heart—like a lump in my chest. Oh, Father,
show me what to do . . . I go on, abysmally lonely. Why
must it be?*

Jim's final trip abroad came in March and April of
1969. Together we traveled to Mexico, Peru, Argentina, Chile, and Brazil. In San Juan, Argentina, twenty-
five college men had a fiesta in our honor. It was a
tremendous gesture of warmth and friendship, something Jim had experienced little of from his own people since June of 1964. He wrote in his journal: *Jim III
and I were guests of honor at a big* fiesta *today. This
was one for the books—bestowing their highest approval, friendship, and honor upon us. I'm sure such a
thing had never before been done in San Juan. It got
pretty rough on us, due to all the toasts—seemed inter-
minable—but of course it's a gesture of friendship. After
all those toasts, they uncorked the champagne—boy, we
were lucky to get out under our own steam. The Spirit
carried us, I guess. I must write more about this his-
toric event. It's this sort of thing that keeps pushing my
insides—makes me sure that I can do a great job down
here,* and that I must. *But how? Where do I find the
people?*

I had never before seen a group of Latin Americans
have such fun with two "gringos." Jim's charismatic
personality had conquered another group of kids,

seven thousand miles from home They didn't know of his exile, nor would they have cared. They only knew that he was interested in them and had traveled seven thousand miles to be their friend.

Kahlil Gibran seemed ever so appropriate:

> *Truth visits us led by the smile of a child and a lover's kiss, and we close the door of our tenderness against her and abandon her as one unclean.*
>
> *The human heart asks succor of us, and the spirit calls us, but we stand as one turned to stone, hearing not nor understanding. And when one hears the cry of his heart and the call of his spirit, we say that such a one is possessed of a madness, and we cleanse ourselves of him.*

E I G H T E E N

Homecoming

JIM'S health was rapidly deteriorating. His journal from 1966 to 1969 records frightening symptoms:

Strange and scary symptoms with my eyes—can't always focus on the television, and see colored spots where I know there aren't any.

Feel I have two lumps in my body. One is in my heart, and one is in my head.

Seizure about 9 p.m. while watching television. Next awareness ambulance—hospital.

Very ill—worst time with my eyes—absolutely no focus possible—then seizure—hospital.

I know something's wrong—my memory very poor—sometimes nonexistent. Cannot remember last two weeks. Frightening . . .

Had my "hay baled" and speech prepared, but I took fifty minutes to present a twenty-minute message. Can't understand what's happening—is it the trauma? Has it been too much? Very scary symptoms.

At times Jim would tremble so violently that we had to hold him down so he could rest. We couldn't stop his insides from shaking, however. In his journals he frequently mentions those terrible, terrifying "inner shakes." They seemed to be triggered by the trauma of his exile. Sometimes they terminated in a violent seizure.

What is one to feel when he holds a convulsing father in his arms? For a good man to die this way seemed a terrible injustice. Could followers of Christ possibly do this to one of their own?

I was searching for answers that only God could give. Perhaps a quote from Omar Bradley, glued to the inside cover of Jim's checkbook, is the best explanation: "We have grasped the mystery of the atom and rejected the Sermon on the Mount. The world has achieved brilliance without wisdom, power without conscience. Ours is a world of nuclear giants and ethical infants. We know more about war than we know about peace, more about killing than we know about living."

If Jim was on the road, with the kids, or otherwise working, his improvement was remarkable. But most of his time was spent at home, and it was not a home for Jim. Maxine's problems were into their fourth decade, and he had no strength left to cope with them. In almost every respect, Jim was a broken man. Many are the nights I sat up with him while he wept.

After five years of living with his tears, tremors, insomnia, convulsions, and emotional pain, we finally got the big news. Jim had cancer. On June 7, 1969, he wrote: *Dr. Beadles came by the room this morning and said I could leave the hospital if I want to. He said to come by his office Monday and by then he'd have the pathologist's report. It sounds fishy and ominous. I know very well that he got the report before he finished the surgery.*

Then, two days later: *To Dr. Beadles' office today. He beat around the bush—finally told me I had a prostatic tumor, already spread to the bladder and urethra. It's a malignancy of a virulent type. I felt sorry for Bob [the doctor]. I told him he didn't need to horse around with me—just to give it to me straight. It's bad! Strange and wonderful—the measure of peace I had. I've felt worse about a broken leg.*

After five weeks of cobalt radiation therapy, there wasn't much left of Jim. Constant nausea, inability to eat or sleep, and those ever-present tremors all worked together to make living one more day a special challenge.

On Halloween, 1969, Jim and Max were jolted once again. Their daughter Sue (Mary Margaret), aged 29, had just undergone a radical mastectomy. Cancer had now struck two of us within five months. The Rayburn family seemed to be living through a night that had no sunrise. Except for one brief entry, Jim stopped keeping a journal after learning of Sue's illness. It seemed to be the final blow, the knockout punch.

183

Upon learning of Jim's impending death, representatives of Young Life invited him to speak at an international staff conference in January 1970 at the Asilomar Conference Grounds, Monterey Peninsula, California. It was to be Jim's first appearance before the staff in six years.

Hours before his speech, Jim seemed on the edge

of dying. His body racked by pain, nausea, and radiation sickness, there seemed to be just no way that he could speak. We in the family were most concerned with the consequences if he went ahead. It was not an audience sympathetic to failure from Jim, and it seemed he was taking a tremendous risk. But there were things he had to say.

At 8:00 a.m. Jim stood before "his people"; he was greeted with a standing ovation. In thankfulness for that brief moment, the tears flowed from my face.

At the time I thought Jim's message to be quite good, maybe exceptional, in light of his circumstances. But I was neither hearing him nor understanding. I was not yet tuned to the realm of Spirit. After the healing touch of Jesus on the blind eyes of my heart, I listened again to Jim's Asilomar message. This time it moved me, made me worshipful and pensive. It was the man's last speaking engagement, and he went out in style. He had started out talking to kids in their own language, and he finished his public work that same way. God alone knows how many "heard" what he was saying.

"Everyone has a right to know the truth about Jesus Christ," Jim told the staff. "They have a right to know who he is, a right to know what he's done for them, a right to know how they relate to that, a right to know him personally. Furthermore they have a right to make their own choice of him.

"Now, if you got in here accidentally, without realizing that that's what Young Life is all about, then you ought to get squared away, or you ought to hunt up the nearest telephone booth and ask for the bus schedule. That's not just what Young Life is all about, that's all that Young Life is all about—Jesus Christ."

Jim's one love was Jesus Christ, and that was the love he had tried to bring to Young Life. In his years in exile, however, he'd seen his little mission flirting with other loves. Jim feared his outfit's newfound emphasis on money, corporate management techniques, papers, forms, policy manuals, and benefit programs. This mad rush to organize, to seek the approval of the institutionalized churches, to elevate theology above relationships—these were areas of grave concern to him. Theology, the science of religion, is an intellectual attempt to systematize the consciousness of God. No one appreciated it more than Jim did. In its place, it is a handmaid of religion. But once elevated into first place, theology becomes a tyrant. In the words of Oswald Chambers, "No one damns like a theologian." Jim's people had theology, but they had still thrown him out and locked the door.

Jim knew his little church of twelve hundred staff people was in the midst of a storm, and there was not much he could do. Having been tossed overboard, he was in some heavy seas himself. He knew one thing though: he knew that if his people's eyes were focused on the Lord, they'd pull through. Jim's last message was a statement, a plea, and a warning. The wolf was at the door, and Jim knew it.

One joyful interlude in these otherwise difficult days gave Jim quite a lift—finding out that Lucia, his Brazilian daughter-in-law, was going to have a baby. "It will be a girl," Jim said, and then he announced to the family that he'd made one last major request to the Father—that he would live to see his granddaughter. None of us thought he had a chance, but if Jim said he'd asked his Father for a green and red zebra, it was wise to get up and prepare the corral.

There was a freshness, a little-boy realness to Jim that endeared him to many. Frequently at the Penrose Cancer Clinic he'd pick out some despondent and pathetic looking person and shout out, "Hi, how's your cancer today?" After the shock wore off, a few engaged in their first open and honest conversation about their illness, exposing their fears and soaking up the warmth of Jim's love.

Thanks to John Miller, Jim was finally given access to Trail West Lodge. There was no place in the world he loved more. At times during his last months, Jim just needed someone to talk to. One night at Trail West, John, the manager, was awakened by a knock on his door. Groggy and confused, John glanced at his clock, saw it was three-thirty in the morning, and assumed he'd been dreaming. After a brief pause, the knocking continued. John struggled to his feet, grabbed a robe, and clumsily made his way to the door. His eyes fell on Jim, leaning against the doorjamb. "Hi, John, don'tcha want some ice cream?" "Yeah," said John, "I've just been lying here wishing someone would ask me that." And the two disappeared down the hallway.

Jim did live to see his granddaughter, Shannon Kathleen. When Lucia and I left the hospital with our newborn baby, we took her straight to Jim's bedside. He held her in his arms but didn't say a thing. Even talking was a fight. But the moment held great significance, for in the eyes of that baby girl, Jim saw that God had honored his final request. Now his time had come.

186

Ten days later, Jim had a sudden burst of energy. He got up, got dressed, arranged transportation, and went to say good-bye to several old friends. Then, on the afternoon of December 7, 1970, while napping, I dreamed that my father had come to the house, sat on the bed, laid his hands on me, and after several minutes, departed. When I awoke, I was informed that he had come and done just as I had dreamed. Late that same evening the nurse called to inform me that Jim had taken a serious turn for the worse. Within twenty minutes I was by his side; it was too late for any final words together. Just that morning he had talked to

Maxine of another dimension. Now, so soon, he was beyond our reach.

Jim had had another seizure, vomited blood, and lapsed into a coma. His breathing was heavy, and an awful "death rattle" was clearly audible. Harlan Harris, a Southern Baptist minister and long-time friend of Jim and Maxine, came to Jim's side immediately. Harlan read aloud a passage from the New Testament, and without opening his eyes, Jim mumbled, "I know that one." It was the only sign of consciousness he gave; he never spoke again.

We had promised my father that he could die at home and that we wouldn't lengthen his final hours in any way. We did not want him to have to fight for each breath, however, so we ordered a tank of oxygen. Morphine was given on schedule.

Seconds turned into minutes, minutes into hours, and hours into days. The only sound was Jim's labored breathing. After forty-eight hours of listening to him fight for each breath, in spite of the added oxygen, I felt I couldn't take much more. I went downstairs and asked God to give me some indication, when the end finally came, that he was there, that Dad was with him, and that things were in his hands.

On the morning of December 11, 1970, after eighty-one hours in a coma, the rhythm of Jim's breathing changed dramatically. He labored to take his last breath, held it briefly, and graduated to his higher destiny. He had slipped beyond the reach of further suffering or pain. Deep sorrow and deep joy blended into one. "Free at last, free at last, thank God almighty, he's free at last."

Within seconds, a flock of birds just outside the open bedroom window burst into song. And they kept on singing as if their little hearts were filled with joy. "An early summer morning," I thought, "not at all like December." And I knew.

The emotional trauma and isolation of Jim's last years contrasted strangely with the hundreds of tributes which poured into Colorado Springs from around the world.

Jim now knows fully what we still know only in part. We rejoice with him. I am grateful for the privilege that was mine to know him, and to experience his unique gift of teaching a group to see Christ, above and beyond all. I pray that today, again, through Jim's death, as through his life, we will focus our attention and message on Christ, above and beyond all else.

Kay McDonald, staff member

So Jim has gone with God. Alleluia!

C. Stacey Woods

The sympathy of me personally and of Inter-Varsity Christian Fellowship to the Rayburn family and to Young Life over the death of Jim Rayburn. He was a godly man whom the Lord greatly used. May the comfort of our Savior be yours this day.

John Alexander, President
Inter-Varsity Christian Fellowship

We thank God for the life and ministry of our beloved brother, Jim. We shall miss him.

William Culbertson,
Moody Bible Institute

We send our deepest sympathies to the Young Life family, especially to Maxine. Rejoicing in all God has brought into being through Jim's vision and commitment.

Bruce Larson, Ralph Osborne,
Heidi Frost, Wally Howard
Faith at Work staff

Am glad Jim Rayburn is now in the arms of Jesus. He was one of the greatest Christians I ever knew, and he had a profound influence on my life. He had suffered a great deal in recent years, but I'm convinced that it is only through suffering that we can share in the glory of Christ. It is now up to us to carry the torch that Jim so courageously carried for so many years.

> *Billy Graham*

The Y.F.C. family extends deep sympathy, and yet rejoices in the triumphant passing of our beloved brother, Jim Rayburn. It is our prayer that his large vision shall find increasing fulfillment.

> *Sam Wolgemuth*
> Youth For Christ

Rayburn's life was an inspiration to all of us. He fulfilled life's noblest purpose in leaving a heritage to the world. It would be impossible to evaluate the immense impact which this man had upon the lives of others.

> *Frank Morrison*
> Governor of Nebraska

Our mutual friend meant more to me than can be expressed. He taught us the practice of love by example. He made Christ a reality, a true companion and friend. Our love and prayers are with his family.

> *Doug Coe*

189

It was sad news to learn that a great man will no longer be among his friends on earth. Jim Rayburn's life expressed the real victory in living for Christ.

> *Albert H. Quie*
> Congressman from Minnesota

How we thank the Lord for the ministry Jim had on our work. He was truly a pioneer for Jesus Christ.

> *Lorne C. Sanny*
> Navigators

Jim realized the necessity of communicating the gospel of Jesus Christ in language intelligible to this generation. He was one of God's tools to shape me for service.

> *George M. Cowan*
> Wycliffe Bible Translators

Jim's passing brings vividly to mind a great summer at Star Ranch in 1950. My life could never be the same again. I am so deeply grateful that I was allowed to know Jim Rayburn.

> *William T. McKenzie*

Jim did something unique in Christian history, I am sure. He was God's instrument for pulling my life out of a confused aimlessness to purpose, enrichment, and love. How I thank God for him! I wish he'd been granted more years of useful, creative work, but *wow,* didn't he give us a whale of a lot?

> *Bob Page*

I am sure there was a great rejoicing when Jim passed on. Many who were there through Jim's teaching were waiting for him. That includes our son, Tom, who went home to the Lord at the age of sixteen while in camp at Star Ranch in 1948.

> *Walter and Jean Henderson*

On the night of February 23, 1952, Jim, under the guidance of the Holy Spirit, spoke to my heart. That night I met my precious Savior. Our little guy, Mark, at five years of age, went to be with his heavenly Father on October 27. He had a rare

blood disease. It is only the Lord who sustains us.
                                    Ron and Emily Huber

My loving sympathy to the Rayburn family and the
Young Life community in this day of common sorrow and grateful remembrance. He who is now
with the Lord he so dearly loved and served, and
whose vision brought into being one of the most
original and dynamic mission projects of our time,
will live on in Christian history as one of the great
saints and evangelical pioneers of this century.
                        John A. McKay,
                        former president of Princeton Seminary

We awoke Sunday, December 13, to find the following article on the front page of the *Colorado Springs
Sun.* It was written by Bill Woestendiek, the editor, in
his column, "Thinking Out Loud."

Jim Rayburn never got his book written, but he
got his life lived and made thousands of other
lives better because of his. Jim died Friday at 61,
and the people of our town, and youth everywhere, lost a good friend.

I was lucky enough to meet and talk with Jim
only last week. He called me and asked me to
come by his house and chat about things he considered important: our town and our young people.

As many of you know, Jim was the founder of
Young Life, an international, interdenominational,
interracial movement that has "turned on for the
Lord" thousands of young people around the
world. Young Life has been described as "friendship evangelism," and has given disinterested
teenagers not only an intelligent look at the Christian faith, but a new outlook on life at a time
when they need it.

191

The organization was founded in Texas in 1938 by a student ministerial assistant who was given the assignment of doing something about teenagers who wouldn't go to church.

That young ministerial assistant, 61 years young, sat in his living room last week, his body racked with the pain of a killing cancer, his eyes bright with joy, and he told me why he started it. . . .

"The kids needed it, they were responsive as the dickens to it, there was nobody else who would do it if I didn't, so by George, I thought I'd take a crack at it."

What a crack that rugged man took at it! In his words, "It's almost too big for its britches now." Today, there are clubs in forty-six states and in many foreign countries.

The story of the growth of Young Life and what it has done for many kids who needed help is an interesting one, but this is about the man who started it all, Jim Rayburn.

"I wanted to talk to you," he told me last week, "because I like what you're trying to do for this town, your fight against drugs, your efforts to help people."

And I wanted to talk to him because he already had done so much for so many people. I asked him if he saw many changes in today's kids.

"It's an entirely different ball game," Jim said. "It's so changed you can't believe it. We've dealt with tough kids all our life. We take them as they come. . . . Rich toughs are harder than poor toughs. . . . But we didn't have any of this drug problem." He shook his head sadly. "Now, you can't believe it."

He straightened up in his chair, grimacing, but his voice was firm. "It's responsible for major changes in our work, but it doesn't change our effort. Any kid on any level, no matter how much of

a smart aleck or how far out he thinks he is . . .
we'll accept him, and we care in terms he can understand. If we can't do it, we'll take the blame."

He lit a cigarette. "They told me I wouldn't live
until last June," he said slowly. "But I had to see
my granddaughter. I didn't say grandchild," he
emphasized, "I prayed for a granddaughter. And
she's beautiful."

Jim's nurse was leaving. "You just keep sweet
now," he told her.

Concerned that we were talking too long, I
asked Jim how he'd sum up his life.

"I was trying to give kids a chance to take a
crack at the Christian faith. This involved either
believing it or not, they're free to make a choice.
But it's hardly fair for nine-tenths of the people to
be making their choice on the basis of some mut-
tonhead college professor's book or something,
with no exposure to it at all. We want to give them
a chance to exercise their option."

Jim exercised his option to the hilt. He died
filled with a concern about people and the problems of our town that worried him more than the
killing pain that racked his body. He wanted to
talk about our problems, and what the *Sun* could
do about them.

193

"You have the guts of a grizzly bear," he told
me, and I shall long treasure that remark. But Jim
was dead wrong. He had it all backwards. He's the
guy who had "the guts of a grizzly bear." I
thought, as he insisted on walking me to my car,
and stood in the sun waving goodbye, that it
would be beautiful if we could do half as much for
as many people as Jim Rayburn did in his all-too-
short young life.

I am grateful that he called me last week. It was
an important afternoon in my life.

NINETEEN
Healing

SHORTLY after Jim's death, Max called on a
local minister. She was in the midst of deep grief,
seeking love, support, and encouraging words.

"He was oblivious to my feelings," she says.
"Mainly, he wanted to talk about the newspaper article that appeared shortly after Jim died. The article
mentioned that Jim had lit a cigarette during the in-
terview. That cigarette was the only thing on his
mind. I left feeling most alone and deeply frustrated. I
had seen my husband die with a broken heart, and in
an hour of need, my minister friend couldn't see past

a cigarette. I guess I decided right then that the time had come to follow my heart."

At sixty years of age, Max decided to take up dancing. She gave herself to that endeavor with an enthusiasm I'd never seen in her before. In short order she was entering dancing competitions from Puerto Rico to California. A couple of her dance instructors were homosexual, and, deeply touched by Maxine's warmth, acceptance, and realness, they decided that their lesbian and homosexual friends should meet her. Before long Maxine's house was filled with society's "trash," people who could come to her and be accepted, people who needed someone to love them as Christ does.

When Max quit trying to live according to the standards of others and gave an ear to the call of her own spirit, she blossomed. As her outcast friends grew in number, she found herself with a purpose, and people who appreciated and needed her. For the first time in years she was happy.

At this critical point in terms of Maxine's healing, she was blasted on the blindside. Word arrived that daughter Sue had inoperable cancer in both lungs; five lesions in one side, two in the other. It didn't seem possible; only thirteen months had elapsed since Jim's death. Sue died on July 3, 1973, at the age of thirty-three after a long, painful, and bravely fought battle against a merciless killer disease.

Before Sue's death, Max had flourished as never before with a renewed determination to find her true self. And she had made such progress! But the trauma of losing her daughter so shortly after losing Jim had been another setback. Fear of the future, that old demon that had followed her so long, began to take control again. Weighed down with grief, unable to understand the pain of the previous ten years, Max turned again to drugs. She wrote:

LONGING

Peace and quiet—for this I longed—
So young,
So immature,
I longed for peace and quiet.
Healthy children played
And made such noise—
I longed for peace and quiet.

The years sped by—
The children grew
And went away.

So now alone
The peace, the quiet that I longed for
Is here.

Now older,
More mature,
I long to hear the children's noise—
The sound that healthy children make in play
Is not a burden—
Cannot be compared to the loudness of the silence
I now endure.

How very much Maxine's spirit, her true self, needed
to be released!

When she was true to herself, Maxine was always a
nonconformist. Her spirit had found an outlet through
poetry and painting, but there had been few around
her, including her husband, with the sensitivity to
"see" and "hear" what she was saying. Christian people usually viewed her as a failure, a rebel, a drug ad-
dict, or at best, an enigma. Affirmation had come to
Max primarily through the local community of artists,
who had noticed her talent and thought her oil paint-
ings worthy of exhibit in the local Fine Arts Center.
Maxine's poetry expressed a side of her that few

could see. Even in the worst years of her illness, she poured out her innermost self to the blank pages of a notebook:

A POEM FOR THE DAY

I like Siamese cats—
And big red apples—
Works of art—
And Spanish castles—

I like fresh baked bread—
Crisp, golden pretzels—
A jet plane—
And Frankfurt am Main—

I dig the fog of London—
And chocolate cake—
Most nonconformists—
And those who think—

I like so many things—
So many places—
Belgium lace—
And a small child's face—

I like so many things—
Like Siamese cats—
And big red apples.

198

If one digs nonconformists, certain religious environments are not fertile soil. And that's sad, for in true Christianity, nonconformity is a must. If God made each snowflake unique, imagine what he did with people! In Christ's true church, there is absolutely no uniformity of personalities, talents, callings, or lifestyles. Without knowing it, Maxine had been searching for the "real thing."

Jim had spent much of his life struggling to please,

or at least not offend, those who conformed to the institutional system. His struggle to mix the old wine
with the new had only confused Max further. When
she dropped out of church, for example, Jim was not
the least bit happy. One can well imagine the frustra-
tion of an artistic, free-spirited, nonconformist woman
trying to find and follow the call of her own spirit, in a
world where many people around her were struggling
to free themselves from strict religious upbringings! A
recurring dream best shows how Max felt: "I was out-
doors, on a high, forested mountain ridge, and there
were lots of people around me. Everybody there was
familiar to me, and I recall they were all very busy.
Everyone was running around looking for something,
and they were oblivious to my presence. Finally, several approached me and said, 'You'd better get busy,
Maxine, there isn't much time.' I said, 'For what,
what's happening?' They said, 'Oh, Maxine, there's
going to be a big, big masquerade party. We're all
going; we're all in it. We're trying to find our costumes so nobody will know who we are. We've got to
have good costumes! Nobody will know us! But Maxine, you're just standing here—don't you want to join
the fun?'

"I said, 'No, look!' and I pointed down to the ground.
We were standing in a beautiful green meadow with
lush strawberries, but people were running around
and trampling them, oblivious of their actions. I was
amazed, angry, and frustrated. I wanted to stand up
tall and put a stop to the whole thing right there! But I
didn't and everyone kept running around, destroying
more berries with every step they took. I tried to pick
a few myself, but remember feeling deeply frustrated.
'This is awful; I can't possibly save these berries by
myself. Somebody has to do something.' "

The religious masquerade had bothered Maxine
ever since her introduction to Jim's world: "I saw peo-

199

ple so busy in their efforts to 'win the world'—holding
meetings, organizing everything, making plans, etc.—
that oftentimes the people closest by were getting
trampled, and no one was noticing. I knew something
was wrong, badly wrong, but I didn't know what the
solution was. It wasn't in my nature to stand up and
tell everyone to take off their masks. I was pretty cov-
ered up myself, and furthermore, I've always hated to
hurt people's feelings.

"The emotional trauma of Jim's last years had
served to convince me that my intuitions had been
right, that I should have listened to them more carefully. Such a realization did wonders for my self-
image; I had a new found self-respect, and I was
being healed."

But Maxine still did not know how to deal with pain.
"It was Sue's death that knocked the train off the
tracks. She was so young and had so much to experience, I just couldn't find an explanation for it. It
seemed that maybe I was being punished for rebel-
ling. I turned again to the only anesthetic I knew."

Max was in and out of drugs, close to herself, then
far removed again, for six years following Sue's death.
Then, in 1979, a crisis threatened. Her heart, every
beat of which had been a miracle for fifteen years,
was acting up and threatening to rupture. In short order, she was also diagnosed as having rheumatoid ar-
thritis with a totally deteriorated hip joint. The doctors
advised a hip replacement, but Max wasn't sure her
heart could take the shock of major surgery. On the
other hand, not to proceed with the operation meant a
wheelchair or being forever bedridden. It seemed a
toss-of-the-coin situation at best.

That same year, Maxine's financial till hit rock bottom. Her only valuable possession was her home. An
immediate move was necessary, but her emotional
state was much too raw to face the numerous details
and decisions.

Once again Maxine reacted to difficult circumstances by attempting to escape them through drugs. In the spring of 1979, while heavily sedated, she suffered a bad fall, cracking her forehead open on the edge of a cement stairway. Several hours later, she called me to say she needed help. I arrived at the scene of a nightmare. The quantity of blood on the porch, floors, and walls was shocking. Mother's head was split open to the bone from her right eyebrow to an inch above her hairline. She was confused; she had lost much blood; and her pulse was very weak. I rushed her to the hospital and had her sewn up in the emergency room (fifty stitches), but I couldn't find a doctor who would admit her. I reluctantly drove her home and put her to bed.

The next day, while heavily sedated once again, Max fell again. I arrived to the same shocking scene, but this time I found her head split open from her eyebrow, up her forehead, and over the top of her skull. It was a twelve-inch gash, open to the bone. Her eyes were black and her body was badly bruised. With the help of Dr. Donna Johnson, a dear friend and gifted psychologist, I admitted mother to the psychiatric ward at Penrose Hospital. It all seemed like a bad dream, for I'd never once felt my mother was mentally ill.

201

How my own faith was being tested! Two years before, my wife, Lucia, and I had found the higher realm, thanks to the grace of God. The Holy Spirit came to live in our hearts and all things became new. I came to understand that what was lacking in so much Christianity was nothing more than this—the Holy Spirit. I found a new power in my prayers, a new hope in my heart, and a new way of seeing things. My mother was the subject of much prayer; I was truly looking for miracles in her life. But with Maxine at the end of her rope, my prayers appeared most ineffective.

Caught in this tangled web of sorrow, drugs, exile, deaths, poor health, and uncertain tomorrows, Maxine finally gave up the fight and surrendered. It was time to heed those "rebellious" intuitions from within. There was nothing more to cling to; she didn't have the strength to be afraid anymore. Afraid of what? She had gotten so low that there wasn't any place lower to fear. At the bottom of life, Max broke. And my little seed of faith, God's seed, really, turned into a giant redwood tree. The Baptizer, the risen Lord Jesus Christ, came to Maxine in his power. Max spent one night in the hospital and checked herself out—*healed!*

T W E N T Y

Dance, Children, Dance

PROPHETS come in different shapes and varied sizes. They are easily recognized in history books, seldom appreciated in their day. Historically, prophets have been unquestionably controversial, and at times, unpardonably hostile. They've always been people who announced, pronounced, and denounced. Most have met with persecution, and an "untimely" death. Like Jim, they have usually been at odds with the established religious system. Prophets are God's messengers, and mankind's enigma; Jim may well have been one.

A former Young Life board member, and dear friend
of Jim, Dr. William F. "Chubby" Andrews, recalls:

> It is with a deep sense of love and great joy that I
> remember Jim and the many happy hours we
> spent together—at the ranches, here at our home
> in Memphis, when I was an intern in Chicago, and
> the time Jim spent a week with me at the hospital.
> I can genuinely say that much of the fruit in my
> own life's work has been by the grace of God
> through the influence Jim Rayburn had upon my
> life.
>
> It is my sincere prayer that those who have a
> love, burden, and concern for young people in
> their hearts, may again recall the enthusiasm,
> zeal, love, compassion, and selflessness that was
> manifested in the life of Jim. Jesus Christ himself,
> who Jim so wonderfully honored, will again be
> glorified and praised as the center of the work of
> Young Life.

One thing is for certain, Jim was earnest to the
core. His heart ached for people who didn't know
Christ in a personal, life-changing way. That earnestness is what sets the man apart, and it also looms as
the greatest challenge to those who would follow him.

I shall never forget a long, hot, miserable day that I
spent with Jim in the interior of Argentina. We had
left Buenos Aires early in the morning on a flight to
Rosario; our purpose was to rendezvous with several
university students who had heard of Jim through an
Argentine exchange student.

Shortly after noon we arrived at the designated
meeting place, an outdoor amphitheatre on the banks
of the Paraná River. There being no trees at that location we sat in the hot sun for more than two hours

awaiting the arrival of our "hosts." No one showed up.

The mosquitoes coming off that river seemed to us like Texas bluejays, and it soon became clear that we had been selected for that day's lunch. The heat and humidity soared to heights that Colorado boys are not accustomed to; I thought we were going to melt, right there in the middle of Argentina. As a young man in his early twenties, I could see no rhyme or reason for our being there. Jim, as one should guess by now, figured we should stick it out; he had really wanted to meet these kids and believed they'd wanted to meet us.

In mid-afternoon, when Jim was just on the verge of giving up, a small group of noisy, boisterous college kids arrived to greet us. They weren't late, by Argentine culture; we'd been early. Being two "gringos" in a foreign land, we had no idea what an Argentine means when he says, "We'll meet you at noon."

For the next three hours, we were grilled with questions about the Vietnam war, American politics, the Roman Catholic Church's domination of South America, and many other complex issues. Neither of us could converse on such topics with our limited Spanish, so we were most dependent on a young American man the students had brought along to translate.

Things couldn't have been more awkward. Our translator was a pugnacious, militant Marxist, who seldom correctly translated a word we'd said. As these Argentine young people looked up to their American friend, our heated conversations with him (never translated) only served to decrease our rapport with the group. We were clearly in a losing situation; it was not an event I ever hope to repeat.

Our flight back to Buenos Aires was delayed; we stood in a miniscule airport from 9:00 P.M. to 3:00 A.M. At 5:00 we were back in our hotel, sunburned, bug-bitten, and exhausted. We both plopped down on the edge of our beds and stared down at our shoes, as if too tired to remove them.

Next thing you know, Jim lifts his head and starts to talk about what a great day it had been, how thankful he felt for the opportunity to know such a great group of kids, and how he hoped God would lead him in spending more time with them in future days. Clearly, he was on a high, and had a heart overflowing with thankfulness. I climbed into bed without saying much, and drifted off to sleep wondering what possessed my father. It was a life-changing question; eight years later I received the answer.

For you, Jim, these words from Theodore Roosevelt:

> It is not the critic who counts, nor the man who points out how the strong man stumbled, or where the doer of deeds could have done them better.
>
> The credit belongs to the man who is actually in the arena; whose face is marred by dust and sweat and blood; who strives valiantly; who errs and comes short again and again; who knows the great enthusiasms, the great devotions, and spends himself in worthy cause; who, at the best, knows in the end the triumph of high achievement; and who, at the worst, if he fails, at least fails while daring greatly, so that his place shall never be with those cold and timid souls who know neither victory nor defeat.

206

One will not follow Jim, nor do the work that he did, on admiration alone. One will never capture Jim inside the pages of policy manuals and committee reports. The Spirit that drove this man cannot be held within the confines of administrative excellence and corporate structure. To systematize Jim is to lose him, and everything he stood for. This issue will serve as the greatest challenge to the organization he left behind, and history makes obvious the danger lurking.

Jim Rayburn was another voice crying in the wilderness, calling "Christians" back to Jesus Christ. His only tool in carrying the life-giving gospel of Christ to the young adults of his generation was faith. He had begun with no job description, no guaranteed salary, few benefits, no organizational plan, few people, and precious little encouragement. But Jim gave to God the only thing God really desires from his people—a yielded life!

Jim took Jesus Christ off the black and white pages of the Bible and placed him there in front of us for all to see. We discovered that we liked him, that he was *good* after all, far better than we'd ever dreamed. Jim helped us to see that Jesus laughed, and that he still laughs, that Christ is also King in the realm of humor. And in our hearts we felt relieved; God seemed closer. Laughing together became a part of worship.

Jim showed us Christ's compassion for the little people: the losers, the drunks, the prisoners, the liars, the cheaters, the weary, and the heavy-laden. And in our hearts we liked that too, for it made us feel that God still cares for such as we.

Jim taught us that we can learn as much about God in climbing a mountain as we're likely to in an hour of church. And in our hearts, we felt lighter; we've all been bored in the sanctuary, but days in the high country are remembered.

207

Jim gave us a purpose, and a dream. And in our hearts, we soared, for we had a reason for our being. We felt we counted somehow, and that felt good. Someone loved and wanted us; his name is Jesus.

Jim led us to Goldbrick, Orien, Long John, No Nose, Pancho, Lowey (our own Liberace), Shelton, Frog, Simmons, "Squinty" McDonald, Bade, and Kay Mac (our own sorority mother). One couldn't find a "crazier," more lovable dozen than those twelve. Then there was Bill Mitchell, always with a late night massage for "the boss," and an ever present skunk, or chipmunk on his shoulders. And there were many more whose memory puts a smile on one's face: Bud "Smiley" Carpenter, Jay "Pavorotti" Grimsted, Thor, Rex, Kaufman, "Rose Bowl" McKasson, "Tough Love" Milliken, the "University of Tennessee Alumni," Roy "The Reverend" Riviere, Charlie and Harriet—"the real McCoys," George "Mr. Laid Back" Sheffer, and so many others. And that's not mentioning the many wives who found the strength to endure such a family. Jim had a stranger group of disciples than Christ himself, and that's saying something. But in the hearts of those who met these people, there's a happy memory. And that's eternal.

Jim taught us to dream, believe, and expect miracles. And he showed us where to look for the source of our power—on our knees. That was hard; in our hearts we rebelled, for we didn't really like to pray as much as he did. But he challenged us, and his example is always in view. Jim seldom did anything that wasn't exciting, so there must be something in prayer we never discovered.

Jim pioneered, led, and pastored a church that behaved as if taken from the pages of Acts. It was a church two thousand years new, a group of strange, diverse, lovable people who came together to sing, laugh, and pray. And how we sang, and how we laughed (and how he prayed!). Those were special times, as those were kingdom times.

While most were chasing financial rainbows, we were feeling thankful just to eat. And when our cereal bowls were running low, and our doubts were running high, those times of song, prayer, and laughter pulled us through. What we had, we shared; and what we didn't have, we also shared. And that's Christ's church!

Jim taught us to see the beauty of the tiny tundra flowers, and to listen to the holy wind blowing through the aspen grove. In the last place Jim's prayers built, Trail West Lodge, the deer still eat from one's hand, and the trees still whisper God's holy message. All who go there come away renewed. It has become one of Young Life's most useful facilities, just as Jim believed it would. One guest, so touched by his stay there, wrote out a check with six figures for the purchase of Woodleaf, Young Life's California resort for America's high school kids.

In essence, Jim was the avant garde leader of a church that grew up around him, a church searching for its New Testament roots. It was a church without a building, but people with a heart. It was a church without an organ, but music was its heartbeat. Outreach was its purpose, and prayer was its foundation. Christ was its Spirit, and Jim was its soul. She was a beautiful bride. May her dance continue through the night, for the "sun" is soon to rise upon her once again.

As for Maxine, hers was not a life of worldly victories. Like most professing "Christians," Max was bound and buried by doubts, fears, and the tyranny of self-condemnation. But deep within her heart, the Spirit of Truth refused to succumb. As surely as Christ called Lazarus from the tomb, so he has done with Maxine. Ironically, Christ set her free from the curse of religion. "There is therefore now no condemnation for those who are in Christ Jesus. For the law of the Spirit of life in Christ Jesus has set you free from the law of sin and of death" (Romans 8:1, 2, NASB). "The faith which you have, have as your own conviction before God. Happy is he who does not condemn himself in what he approves" (Romans 14:22, NASB). "It was for freedom that Christ set us free; therefore keep standing firm and do not be subject again to a yoke of slavery" (Galatians 5:1, NASB).

May the lessons learned by Max be of benefit to many. Each of us must listen to our own intuitions, not the value judgments of others. The kingdom of God is discovered within; it cannot be found by religious adherence to creeds, codes, and laws. So many "Christians" are so entangled by their religion that they've little hope of finding Christ. These folks have not yet faced their ego, their fears, and their pride, nor have they listened to the call of their spirit.

Those who can face themselves, and the ensuing shock to one's pride, have been promised a great treasure—the Divine Comforter will come and take the hurt and shame away. And that's what true Christianity is all about! The time has come for Christians to wake up and realize that they are fully equipped children of the King, whole and wholly acceptable in the eyes of the Father. There is no place for sin-consciousness and self-condemnation.

Without the Holy Spirit, who is the essence of Christ, we are left with a religious masquerade. Religion kills; the Spirit brings life. The time has come to take off our religious masks, be who we truly are, and experience the warmth of his sweet sunshine on our bare, naked souls. And when we dance together in our spiritual nakedness, perhaps we will come to understand—*Christ has set us free! Alleluia!*

Dance, children, dance!

210

FATHER, it is finished. I give you back the laughs, the tears, the lonely hours, and the precious insights you have given me. May these words go forth to bless, heal, and inspire other lives, bringing them to a living consciousness of their oneness with you.